EASY SOLUTIONS: COLOR MIXING

How to Mix the Right Colors for the Subject Every Time

Watercolor

EASY SOLUTIONS: COLOR MIXING

How to Mix the Right Colors for the Subject Every Time

Watercolor

M. Stephen Doherty

Quarry Books
Gloucester, Massachusetts

First published in the United States of America by
Quarry Books, an imprint of Rockport Publishers, Inc.
33 Commercial Street
Gloucester, Massachusetts 01930-5089
Telephone: (978) 282-9590
Fax: (978) 283-2742

Distributed to the book trade and art trade
in the United States by
North Light Books, an imprint of F & W Publications
1507 Dana Avenue
Cincinnati, Ohio 45207
Telephone: (800) 289-0963

Other distribution by
Rockport Publishers, Inc.
Gloucester, Massachusetts 01930-5089

ISBN 1-56496-417-5

10 9 8 7 6 5 4 3 2 1

Design: Laura Herrmann Design
Cover Artwork: Laura Herrmann Design
Watercolor Backgrounds: H. A. Lind

Printed in Hong Kong by Midas Printing Limited

Additional images credited as follows:

MAY FLOWERS (DETAIL) Deborah L. Chabrian, 11" x 13" (28 CM x 33 CM), PAGE 2

MORNING SHOPPERS, DINAN Robert A. Wade, 11" x 8" (28 CM x 20 CM), PAGE 5

VENICE I Jean Grastorf, 28" x 20" (71 CM x 51 CM), PAGE 6

FRESH EGGS Sharon Weilbaecher, 39" x 28" (99 CM x 71 CM), PAGE 10

Acknowledgments

My thanks first go to the artists who have generously provided the information

and photographs that make this book valuable.

Next, I want to acknowledge the creative contributions of the editors, designers,

and marketing staff at Rockport Publishers.

To my parents, Chic and Dot Doherty, I express my appreciation for a lifetime

of support and encouragement.

Finally, I extend my heartfelt thanks to my wife, Sara, and our children, Clare and Michael.

CONTENTS

INTRODUCTION
Color Choices in the Studio

For those who have never tried it, watercolor seems like an easy medium to master. After all, the only materials needed are a sheet of paper, a brush, and a few tubes of paint; and the only technique to learn is stirring water into paint. But after beginners make a few paintings with garish green trees, dark black rocks, muddy brown water, and ominous gray skies, they realize there is more to handling watercolor than they ever imagined.

The most important lesson novices must learn is that the successful use of watercolor depends on the proper selection and mixture of tube colors. The decision of what colors to choose and how to mix them makes the difference between a glowing, vibrant painting and a dull, muddy mess!

The purpose of this book is to provide users with some practical tips on choosing and mixing tube colors. The twelve artists who have contributed to this book offer an enormous amount of information about color choices and color mixtures that can be helpful to any watercolorist, beginner or advanced. Each artist details the selection of pigments, the combinations of colors on their palettes and on the surface of their paintings, and the steps they take to avoid problems.

You'll find that the artists each have very different approaches to color—some of which seem to conflict with others. Skip Lawrence extols the virtues of opaque colors such as cerulean blue and yellow ochre, while Jean Grastorf cautions against using anything but transparent, staining colors like phthalo blue and Hansa yellow deep. Both artists use color mixtures that work beautifully with their respective painting techniques. Lawrence seeks colors that sink into the paper and create soft, rich landscape forms; Grastorf features staining colors that she can pour in layers to establish glowing light in a floral arrangement.

non-staining watercolors

As you read each chapter and understand why the artists create their own color mixtures, you'll gain an understanding of watercolor paints that will help you formulate your own creative approach to the medium. You may decide to copy Lawrence's palette, or you may prefer to combine some of his colors with ones Grastorf recommends. As long as you are in control of the medium and are achieving the results you want, you're making the correct color mixtures for your paintings.

As a way of introducing the options available to you, I've painted two columns of colors that seem almost exactly alike. I mixed two separate sets of colors to get the same orange, green, brown, and purple. You might conclude, then, that any combination of colors gives the same results. But if you look at the columns to the left and right of the matching columns, you'll see that, when I painted over the original color mixtures or dampened the original squares, the results were quite different.

The reason for the differing results is that I painted one column with mixtures of pigments that don't stain the fibers of the paper and the adjacent column with all staining colors. The non-staining colors quickly mixed with the layers of paint applied over them and easily lifted off the paper when they were dampened. The staining colors, on the other hand, didn't budge. So the staining properties of colors are important to the way they mix.

You'll see in the color workshop sections that the featured artists also concern themselves with complementary colors, synthetic and organic pigments, particulating colors, harmonious tones, and color temperatures. These are just a few of the characteristics you'll want to know about as you choose your palette.

You may be concerned that all this technical information will get in the way of enjoying the creative potential of the medium. It's true that you'll need to digest a lot of material at first. But as you work with colors, you'll get to know them so well that you'll soon have an instinctive understanding of how to mix them. You'll come to have your favorite tube colors, as each of the featured artists does, and you'll know just how to combine them to paint that hybrid rose, copper kettle, or distant mountain.

watercolors that stain the fibers of the paper

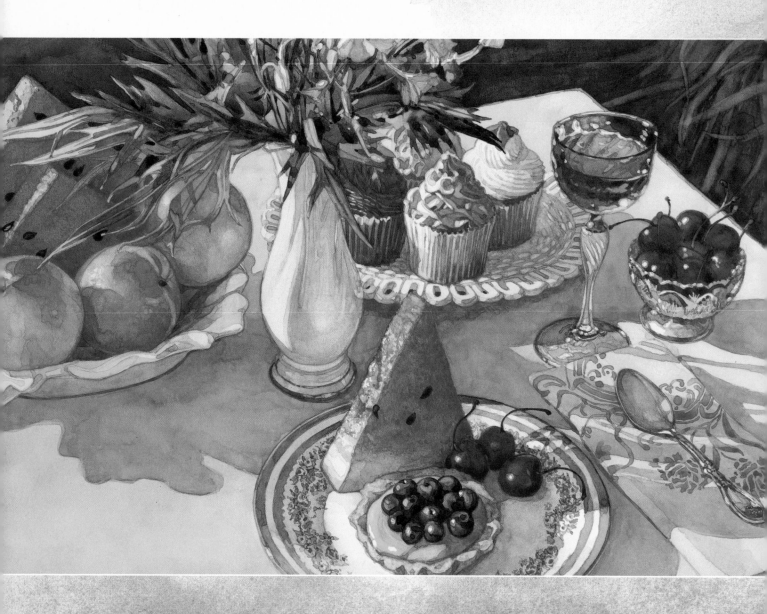

SUMMER DESSERT *Deborah L. Chabrian*, 11" x 13" (27.9 CM X 33 CM)

Color

Mixing

for

Still Lifes

S till-life painting is a process of working with the subtle relationships between the shapes of objects, the textures and surfaces that identify them, and the colors that bring them together. It involves selecting one piece because it is tall and thin, another because it has a shiny surface, and a third because it can be laid between to connect the two objects. And during the painting process, still-life painting means repeating colors, adjusting values, and balancing intense pigments with soft ones. If the painter includes a bright red bottle on the left side of the picture, he or she needs to work some of that same red pigment into the wooden box on the right. Otherwise, the painting will seem awkward and unbalanced.

The three artists featured in this section explain how they achieve those subtle relationships by controlling the mixtures of colors they select for their palettes. All three work directly from observations of pears, apples, checkered fabrics, and other objects that are right in front of them. They challenge themselves to use what they see—the exact colors, shapes, and arrangements—while interpreting their observations in very personal ways. That is, they make note of the real colors in nature but adjust them in an individual manner.

Daryl Bryant mixes a lot of water with her tube colors and lets each color flow into the others on the watercolor paper. She shows you how she maintains the soft edges of the pears, apples, and cloth during the early stages of the painting process, and then adds hard edges toward the end. That combination of hard and soft edges helps to unify the picture, blend the colors, and create an appealing watercolor.

Deborah L. Chabrian also uses techniques that lend harmony to the colors in her still life, but she uses different paints and paper than Bryant. She seals and tones her smooth paper with one color (in the case of her demonstration painting, yellow ochre), which then mixes with all the other layers of paint. This process allows her to distinguish objects with the slightest shifts toward red, orange, blue, or green.

Denise Lisiecki is much less direct in mixing and applying colors, but she too aims for balance and harmony between pigments. She first makes careful studies of the way each pigment performs before applying it to the watercolor paper. This approach helps her decide how to use both complementary and analogous colors to capture the vitality and richness of what she observes.

SUN-BLEACHED SHELL *Daryl Bryant*, 22" X 15" (55.9 CM X 38.1 CM)

Building on Harmonious Colors

"I love quick, gestural strokes of transparent color that suggest the appearance of real objects, people, and places. But the only way to know all those active marks will come together in a successful painting is to plan ahead."

— **Daryl Bryant**

Daryl Bryant applies strokes of fluid color onto a sheet of watercolor paper already made damp by preliminary washes of soft, harmonious colors. The colors blend and remain glowingly transparent. The artist mixes most of the colors on the paper itself to keep them from becoming muddy. This technique allows her to incorporate almost any color—opaque or transparent—but she limits herself to colors that are close to each other on the color wheel or are blended from the same limited number of tube colors.

Throughout the painting process, Bryant makes a conscious effort not to apply washes of color that are too intense or to bring out the details of objects too early in the painting process. She paints large, transparent shapes before establishing the small, opaque details.

Bryant completes her paintings in one sitting so that the colors won't completely dry into the fibers of the watercolor paper until she is satisfied with the picture. Until that point, she is able to manipulate the colors, values, and edges of the painting. "I set aside the time I need and turn the answering machine on so I can devote my full attention to the painting until it is finished," she explains. "If I look at the picture a couple of days later and find it needs a lot of adjustments, I'm likely to just toss it out and start a new painting. An overworked watercolor loses the vibrancy of the colors and the vitality of the brush strokes."

Paintings in this chapter by Daryl Bryant

(OPPOSITE) CUP OF TEA 22" X 15" (55.9 CM X 38.1 CM)
(TOP) BEAN JUG 15" X 22" (38.1 CM X 55.9 CM)
(CENTER) SUN-BLEACHED SHELL 22" X 15" (55.9 CM X 38.1 CM)
(BOTTOM) CHINESE VASE 15" X 22" (38.1 CM X 55.9 CM)

Getting Started

Cadmium Red · Hooker's Green Dark · Winsor Yellow · Sap Green · French Ultramarine Blue · Winsor Violet · Antwerp Blue · Burnt Sienna · Alizarin Crimson · Permanent Rose · Cadmium Orange · Yellow Ochre · Cadmium Yellow · Manganese Blue · Cobalt Blue · Cerulean Blue · Cobalt Violet

Palette

Bryant avoids earth colors because they look chalky when they become thick. When she finds herself repeating the same colors, she changes her palette or technique for applying color. Likewise, she switches from horizontal to vertical formats so each painting has its own problems and opportunities.

Favorites: *Manganese blue and permanent rose.*

Brushes

Bryant uses large flat brushes for the initial washes of color, and large round brushes for the rest of the painting. Toward the end of the process, she uses smaller round brushes, but even these are relatively large.

Favorites: *1 1/2" flat brush made from natural and synthetic hairs; round brushes in sizes #18 and #20.*

Surface

Bryant uses Winsor & Newton paper. She dampens the paper, stretches it on Gatorboard or foam board covered with contact paper, and staples the two together. She applies fluid mixtures of paint that saturate the paper. This dampness helps her maintain soft edges and saturated colors until later in the process.

Favorite: *Winsor & Newton paper.*

Bryant's studio is in a Craftsman-style building that was originally constructed as a private residence and was subsequently divided into small offices. Despite the limited space, she appreciates the privacy and historic setting.

Bryant places the board holding the watercolor paper in a painting easel so she can work standing up, or props it against a drawing horse so she can sit and look at the developing image. She keeps the windows covered to prevent sunlight from changing the illumination on the painting surface. Artificial lights are focused on her subjects and paper.

To determine the composition and proportions of a full-scale watercolor, Bryant makes thumbnail sketches of her subjects. Along with the two or three compositional sketches, she makes notations about the various colors she might use in creating a painting. All of that information helps her make a full-scale, freehand pencil drawing on the stretched watercolor paper.

The first washes of color Bryant applies to the paper are light in value, allowing her to establish a "road map" for the rest of the painting. Those fluid washes also dampen the surface so that subsequent applications of color are intense and soft-edged. As she paints layers of more intense colors, Bryant works around the entire picture so one area doesn't dominate the others.

Building on Harmonious Colors

1 ▶

Bryant makes small watercolor sketches and color studies in her sketchbook to evaluate the layout, compositional possibilities, and colors. She considers both a vertical and a horizontal format for the painting, and makes a gray-and-white value sketch to check the arrangement of values.

diluted
color washes

▲ 2

The artist makes a larger drawing on the stretched 140 lb cold-pressed watercolor paper and applies the first diluted washes of harmonious color with 1¼" and 2" flat brushes. She uses Antwerp blue for the background, brightens the light-struck areas of the vase with Winsor violet and a touch of permanent rose, and washes Hooker's green dark into the area of the tablecloth.

ADVICE FROM THE ARTIST

Think of the painting process as a search for the right colors and values. Try to focus on the planes of color shapes made up of dark, light, and middle values rather than spaces that need to be filled in.

Daryl Bryant

Continuing to develop the basic shapes, Bryant uses Winsor violet, Antwerp blue, and permanent rose for the vase. She pulls some of the Antwerp blue from the background to darken the shadowed side of the vase. She moves paint from one area to another to make color connections, and lightly touches the hard edges with a brush dipped in water to soften those edges.

 4

Continuing to use large flat and round brushes, Bryant applies cadmium red to the apples, then drops in some Winsor yellow, cadmium orange, and manganese blue. She establishes the shade of the pears with burnt sienna and yellow ochre; pulls together the mass of leaves with Winsor yellow, cobalt green, and ultramarine blue; and adds permanent rose and alizarin crimson for warmth and variation.

5

Bryant applies a wash of permanent rose to intensify the vase color while keeping a bright tone, and then adds a mix of Winsor violet and cobalt blue to the wet surface. She works the background shadow with Antwerp blue and Winsor violet, pulling some of the Antwerp blue into the tablecloth to darken its value.

6

Bryant now uses less water to dissolve the paint so she can "punch up" the color with stronger applications of pigment. She also uses slightly smaller brushes and pays more attention to details as she shapes the teapot and cup. She paints a minimal amount of calligraphy on those two objects using ultramarine blue, and darkens the leaves with a mixture of ultramarine blue, Hooker's green, and Winsor yellow.

7

The artist pulls the green into the foreground to show the fringed edge of the checkered cloth, and darkens the shadows on the left side. She also darkens the blue background to help the flowers stand out more distinctly.

Color Mixing Workshop

Value Study

A quickly painted value study like this one helps Bryant determine how she will use the colors in the painting.

Staining Colors

Bryant begins her demonstration using Antwerp blue, Winsor violet with a touch of permanent rose, and Hooker's green dark—three intense, staining colors that work well together because they are kept transparent and damp.

Antwerp blue

Winsor violet & permanent rose

Hooker's green dark

One of the controlling ingredients in any color mixture is the water added to the pigments while they are on the palette, or when they are stroked across the damp watercolor paper. The

> *The more water added to the tube colors, the more transparent they become.*

more water added to the tube colors, the more transparent they become; and the more moisture on the paper's surface, the more deeply the colors will sink into the fibers and become soft. Conversely, when very little water is mixed on the palette or when the paint is applied to bone-dry paper, the colors will become dense and either translucent or completely opaque.

Daryl Bryant demonstrates how transparent, opaque, and staining colors can all be made light, soft, and luminous by

(ABOVE) BRASS POT 11" X 15" (28 CM X 38.1 CM)
(OPPOSITE) RUSSIAN SHAWL 22" X 15" (55.9 CM X 38.1 CM)

keeping them moist through the painting process. That technique allows her to use a wider range of color mixtures than would be possible with drier applications of paint.

Note that Bryant does not thin her paints so much that the colors become faint and wispy. She uses lots of paint, stirs it thoroughly in the water, and applies it to the damp paper with a well-charged brush. The resulting shapes are soft-edged and transparent, but they are not timid.

Thicker Mixtures of Colors

The artist is able to continue using thicker mixtures of the same three colors because the paper is wet enough for the pigments to blend together and sink into the fibers.

Layering over Dried Paint

Here, Bryant paints the Winsor violet after the Antwerp blue and Winsor violet have dried. Notice that instead of blending into a harmonious color, the combination yields rather dark, gray colors.

Blending Harmonious Colors

Bryant achieves wonderful effects by blending harmonious colors while they are still wet. She paints the apple by first applying cadmium red and then dropping in Winsor yellow, cadmium orange, and manganese blue.

Balancing Related Colors

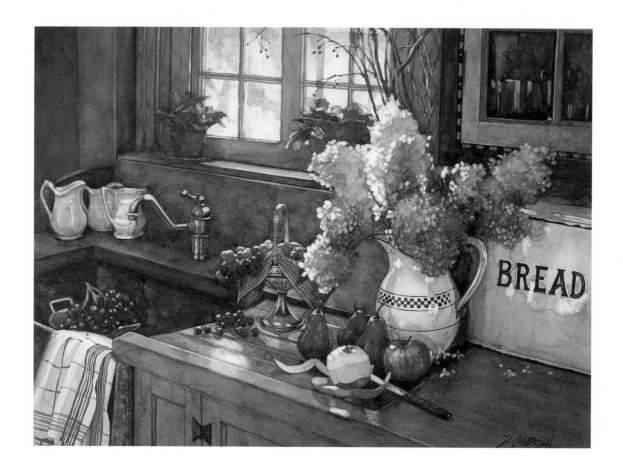

"I don't need paints from all over the palette to get clear distinctions
between colors in the paintings I do on hot-pressed paper.
In fact, when I work within a limited range of harmonious tones,
the slightest shifts in color become much more apparent."

— Deborah L. Chabrian

One of the most critical aspects of Deborah L. Chabrian's technique is working with a limited numbers of colors, especially muted reds, blues, and ochres. She mixes those harmonious tones by allowing four or five colors to blend together on her palette, so that each new combination begins with the colors already in use. This method is a bit like using some starter bread dough saved from one batch to make the next loaf.

With her colors confined to a limited range of intermixed pigments, Chabrian is able to maximize the subtle differences between those colors. A slight shift toward red, blue, or yellow becomes more obvious than if she were to use completely separate tube colors for every shape within her picture.

Another important component is the smooth paper on which Chabrian paints. The polished surface of hot-pressed paper absorbs paint slowly, so particles of pigment separate and cling to the edges of shapes as they dry. The dried pigment gives the open areas a mottled look and forms a thin line around the painted shapes. Furthermore, because so much of the pigment sits on the surface of the paper, the artist can more easily soften edges and lighten values than she could on cold-pressed or rough paper. She can enhance these characteristics of the paper by mixing colors with Chinese white to make them opaque and to seal the paper. The colors then take on a milky, tinted look.

Paintings in this chapter by Deborah L. Chabrian

(OPPOSITE) MY KITCHEN WINDOW 16 ¼" X 21" (41.3 CM X 53.3 CM)
(TOP) DUTCH STILL-LIFE 15" X 19" (38.1 CM X 48 CM)
(CENTER) SUMMER MORNING 14" X 14" (36 CM X 36 CM)
(BOTTOM) SUMMER DESSERT 11" X 13" (28 CM X 33 CM)

Getting Started

Permanent Rose Naples Yellow Raw Sienna Burnt Umber Hooker's Green Light Gamboge Burnt Sienna Alizarin Crimson Cobalt Blue Cadmium Red Deep Cobalt Green Yellow Ochre Cobalt Turquoise Lemon Yellow Raw Umber Cobalt Green

Palette

Chabrian spreads colors around in the slotted compartments of a John Pike palette. She then pulls them into the central mixing area, where she makes up large batches of the colors she expects to use.

Favorites: *Alizarin crimson, Naples yellow, cobalt turquoise (sometimes mixed with Naples yellow), Payne's gray, and Chinese white.*

Brushes

Chabrian uses Isabey squirrel brushes in sizes #6 and #8, Raphäel kolinski sable round brushes in sizes #000 up to #10, and Winsor & Newton Series 239 synthetic round brushes in sizes #1 to #12.

Favorite: *Isabey squirrel, sizes 00, 2, and 6; Raphäel kolinski sable round, sizes 2 and 4.*

Surface

Chabrian usually paints on Strathmore Bristol 4-ply board, which she purchases in 20" x 30" (50.8 cm x 76.2 cm) sheets and cuts to the size of the intended painting. When painting outdoors, she sometimes works on Lanaquarelle hot-pressed paper.

Favorite: *Strathmore Bristol 4-ply board.*

Chabrian warns that hot-pressed paper may seem difficult to work with at first. "The first layer of colors don't stain the fibers of paper as they would with cold-pressed or rough paper. For that reason, the second and third washes can reactivate the first ones and cause the colors and edges to change. It took me a lot of practice to become comfortable with the paper."

Because the pigment never completely settles into the fibers of the paper, Chabrian is able to start painting with broad washes of color and gradually sharpen edges as she would if painting with oil paints. "I save the white shapes by covering them with frisket, block in the large areas of light color, and then break those into smaller and darker forms without worrying about losing my lighter values or clean edges," she says.

Chabrian makes a point of using one color to dominate the picture, two others to play secondary roles in the composition, and splashes of other colors throughout the picture. "For example, I was thinking about the earthy reds that became the focus of attention in the still life shown here in stages of development," she explains. "The ochres cover more of the paper, but it's those reds that grab the viewer's attention, followed by the whites, blues, and greens."

Balancing Related Colors

1 ▶

Chabrian makes a detailed pencil drawing of the still life and applies liquid frisket to preserve the white paper in certain areas. She then works pale, warm washes of yellow ochre, Chinese white, reds, and blues over the entire sheet of Bristol board. The first washes of harmonious colors seal the paper so it won't be stained by subsequent colors.

2 ▲

Still working the entire paper, Chabrian paints pale, warm washes of yellow ochre mixed with Chinese white, and adds small amounts of reds and blues. She then establishes general areas of color with loose, broad washes of reds, greens, blues, and ochres.

ADVICE FROM THE ARTIST

Always have a good amount of pigment in your brush when you touch it to the surface of hot-pressed paper. Too much water in the mixture may cause you to lift off paint when you're trying to lay more on.

squirrel brush

Deborah L. Chabrian

3

The artist begins to get more specific about colors and values, painting pale blues and greens in the areas of reflected light and shadow. She allows the colors to mix spontaneously on the paper to create color harmony and the "beautiful accidents of watercolor."

4

Chabrian now makes an effort to paint the exact appearance of each object, using a hair dryer to speed up the drying time and a stiff bristle brush to remove paint where she needs to lighten values and soften highlights.

5

She begins to add interest in the textures and patterns by covering most of the painting with tracing paper and then splattering paint from the edge of a stiff toothbrush onto the uncovered areas. She splatters cobalt blue, Payne's gray, alizarin crimson, and raw umber into the shadows for variations of purples and blues.

6 ▶

Chabrian removes the frisket and begins to paint the details and darkest values in the picture. She tries not to finish everything to the same degree because she finds it more interesting if some areas are less well defined than others.

◀ **7**

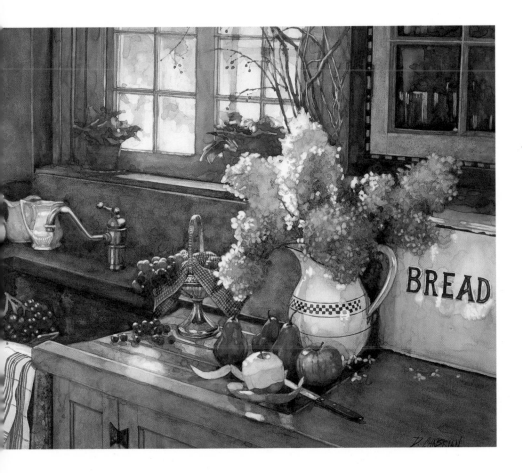

She washes warm colors over the flowerpot in the window, and paints darker tones into the light areas near the board under the grapes. After she adds a few dark touches here and there, she decides the painting is finished and paints her signature.

Color Mixing Workshop

Different Color Mixtures

Chabrian painted all four of these watercolors with mixtures of cobalt blue, ultramarine blue, permanent rose, yellow ochre, and Chinese white. Notice how the different mixtures change the presentation of the same object.

The magic trick Deborah L. Chabrian can teach you is how to get the maximum effect from a few color mixtures. To come up with

> *The magic trick Deborah L. Chabrian can teach you is how to get the maximum effect from a few color mixtures.*

all the reds, blues, yellows, greens, purples, oranges, and grays she needs to complete her still-life paintings, she uses just a few well-chosen tube colors. She works with yellow ochre, raw sienna, permanent rose, Chinese white, and three blues to perform that magic.

Chabrian offers another illustration of the surprising things you can do with a few tube colors. Using a warm and a cool blue (cobalt and ultramarine, respectively), one red, one yellow, and Chinese white, she paints the same still-life object four times. The subtle shifts in mixtures and the changing placements of the colors have a dramatic impact on the resulting images.

All of this should give you a sense of freedom in the way colors can be mixed and applied to your paintings. Chabrian shows how to create your own unique paintings with just the slightest shifts in color, value, and placement. Whether you select the same palette or one that suits your own preferences, the impact will be the same.

Subtle Distinctions

Chabrian achieves subtle distinctions by mixing colors with Chinese white and applying them over a tone of yellow ochre. She paints the central panel with yellow ochre, adding mixtures of raw sienna and permanent rose to the top. To the bottom, she adds mixtures of Winsor blue, cobalt blue, and ultramarine blue.

permanent rose

raw sienna

yellow ochre

Winsor blue & cobalt blue

ultramarine blue

(OPPOSITE) MAY FLOWERS 11" X 13" (28 CM X 33 CM)
(ABOVE) LATE SUMMER FLOWERS 16" X 12" (41 CM X 30 CM)

Shaping Objects with Color

"Painting with watercolor can be compared to laying sheets of colored cellophane on a light box. Each new color combines with those underneath and blocks out a little more of the light coming from within the box."

— **Denise Lisiecki**

Although watercolor paints don't perform exactly like layers of cellophane, Denise Lisiecki's analogy helps in understanding how each new color applied to the watercolor paper affects the developing painting. The choice of color, manner of application, and sequence of layers alters the light penetrating through the paint and reflecting off the white paper.

Lisiecki finds color charts helpful in selecting the right colors for each new mixture. She makes these herself by painting each color full strength at one end of a horizontal line, and

then gradually diluting it as she extends the line. The charts show her not only what each color looks like and how transparent it is, but also the variations that exist between brands. One company's cadmium yellow differs slightly from the cadmium yellow manufactured by other companies.

All of this information about transparent and translucent colors helps Lisiecki establish the three-dimensional appearance and surface texture of the still-life objects in her setups. To create these convincing illusions, she establishes the shadows by layering the colors she has chosen over a carefully drawn pattern on the

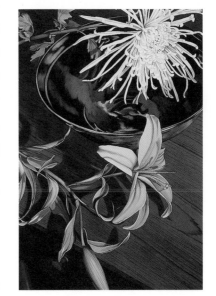

watercolor paper. Lisiecki uses her remarkable command of the watercolor language to communicate to viewers what she finds curious, amusing, elegant, disturbing, or joyous about the pieces she depicts. She chooses still-life objects that represent something she wants to share with other people; they may capture the memory of someone who has died, recall artifacts of a foreign culture, or celebrate appealing forms that complement one another.

Paintings in this chapter by Denise Lisiecki

(OPPOSITE) VIEW OF THE STUDIO 21¼" X 15½" (54 CM X 39.4 CM)
(TOP) IRIS IN SHADOWS 21" X 27" (53.3 CM X 68.6 CM)
(CENTER) WATER CONTAINERS 27½" X 38¾" (69.9 CM X 99 CM)
(BOTTOM) CHRYSANTHEMUM IN BLACK BOWL 48" X 32" (121.9 CM X 81.3 CM)

Getting Started

Schmincke Madder Carmine

W & N Alizarin Crimson

W & N Cotman Sap Green

Rowney Alizarin Green

Schmincke Indigo

Sennelier Lemon Yellow

Rose Dore

Schmincke Neutral Tint

W & N Davy's Gray

Schmincke Cadmium Yellow

W & N Van Dyke Brown

Hooker's Green Light

Schmincke Light Sepia

Schmincke Lamp Black

Palette

Lisiecki squeezes the colors into plastic or porcelain dishes. By the time she completes a painting, she usually has five or six dishes of paint.

Favorites: *Madder carmine and alizarin green. If you find alizarin green too intense, use it over greens that need more vitality, like Hooker's green light.*

Brushes

Lisiecki uses a wide brush to apply water in a controlled manner, and adds the paint with a size #6 or #8 round Kolinski sable brush. These brushes hold a large amount of color, release it gradually as the artist applies pressure, and then come back to a point.

Favorites: *Size #6 round kolinski sable brushes.*

Surface

Lisiecki has tried a number of papers, but has found Arches the best in accepting a lot of paint before the colors start to become opaque. Arches also releases paint when she needs to lighten certain areas.

Favorite: *Arches 140 lb cold-pressed paper, cut from large rolls.*

Lisiecki paints standing at a large drafting table. She usually tilts the table back at a 45-degree angle, but she lays it flat when applying a wash to a large area and raises it to a vertical position when striving for a thin layer of color. To the side of the table, she sets up her still life, illuminated by spotlights that she can move to create different patterns of light and shadow. Lisiecki works from life, not photographs.

Lisiecki arranges and rearranges objects until the selection and composition satisfy her. She is guided both by the message she wants to convey and by the relationship of shapes, colors, patterns, spaces, and textures. When she is finally satisfied with the setup, she makes a thumbnail sketch in pencil to evaluate the balance of shapes and values.

Lisiecki then does a scale drawing of the intended painting so she can make a final determination of the placement and two-dimensional rendering of each object. She transfers the lines of the final drawing to a sheet of watercolor paper taped to her drafting table. She never soaks the entire sheet of paper, but rather paints one shape with clear water before applying paint to that portion of the paper.

Shaping Objects with Color

 1

Lisiecki staples a sheet of Arches 140 lb cold-pressed paper to a board and carefully draws the outlines of the shapes of her still-life subjects with a 2H graphite pencil. She works freehand (rather than from a traced drawing), referring to the objects themselves and her thumbnail sketch of the overall composition.

 2

Using Schmincke neutral tint, she paints the shadows established by the folds of the fabric. Because of its purple-gray tone, neutral tint works well in establishing both the warm shadows of the white fabric and the red checks. If Lisiecki were to use green, red's complement, she wouldn't be able to carry the shadows from the red checks into the folds of the white checks.

3

After painting the pear shapes with clear water, Lisiecki floats cadmium yellow light into those shapes to establish the base of a warm inner glow. She paints the same yellow on the apple shapes to give the green apples a cool yellow tint, and adds a translucent layer of Schmincke madder carmine to the lighter checks of the fabric.

Denise Lisiecki

 4

Lisiecki uses Rowney alizarin green—which she considers the closest tube color to a pure green—to shade the red pears. She will later paint the pears with Schmincke madder carmine. She tints the green apples with Winsor & Newton mauve because that color darkens its complement, yellow, in the green used for the apples.

 5

The artist layers Schmincke madder carmine once over the pears in the foreground and twice over the pear in the background, allowing the paper to dry completely before painting the second layer. She applies Cotman sap green to the apple on the right. Next Lisiecki paints an opaque layer of Schmincke madder carmine over the darker checks. She then adds Winsor & Newton Davy's gray and Schmincke madder carmine inside the silver bowl.

6

Lisiecki washes another layer of Schmincke madder carmine over the pears, and paints an additional layer of Cotman sap green on the apples. She applies Schmincke madder carmine, Winsor & Newton Davy's gray, and Cotman sap green to the silver bowl.

7

Lisiecki washes the apples in the foreground with Cotman sap green and, while the paint is still wet, tips in Winsor & Newton rose carthame to create the reddish orange reflections on the silver bowl.

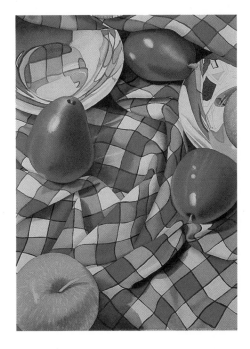

▲ **8**

As Lisiecki refines the painting, she paints thin lines between the checks using Schmincke indigo; the darker areas of the green apples with Rowney alizarin green; the dark areas of the pears with Winsor & Newton alizarin crimson; and the darker areas of the bowls with Schmincke lamp black.

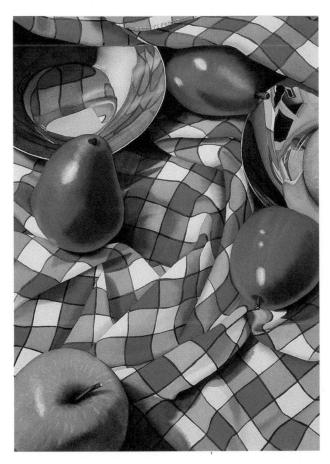

◀ **9**

Lisiecki feels the colors need to be intensified, so she adds a wash of cadmium yellow light to the pears and alizarin green to their shadows. She also creates the reflections in the silver bowls with Winsor & Newton Davy's gray and a mixture of that gray with black.

Color Mixing Workshop

Three-Dimensional Appearance

Lisiecki uses several tube grays to establish the three-dimensional appearance of objects. For the folds of the checkered fabric, she first paints a neutral tint, a gray that has a purple cast.

Metallic Color

To create the metallic look of the silver bowl, Lisiecki first paints washes of Davy's gray, a tube color that leans toward a cool black, and then adds lamp black to finish up the painting.

Denise Lisiecki applies watercolor in distinct layers, with each color wash being allowed to dry thoroughly before the next is applied. That procedure allows the artist to slowly build up the surface of her pictures, gradually increasing the intensity of the color and the illusions of depth and dimension.

> *Denise Lisiecki applies watercolor in distinct layers, with each color wash being allowed to dry thoroughly before the next is applied.*

Lisiecki points out a few things that you might not think about when mixing colors. First, she shows the benefit of underpainting colors that will shift the final layers of paint toward a particular color (in this case, yellow) or toward a warm or cool tone. Next, she demonstrates how painting more than one layer of the same color will increase the intensity of that color shape. Finally, she shows how the use of complementary colors will build shadows.

Because this approach depends on careful planning and a

thorough knowledge of color relationships, it is helpful to make sketches and paint value studies, to keep color charts, and try out color combinations on test swatches of watercolor paper before adding them to a developing painting.

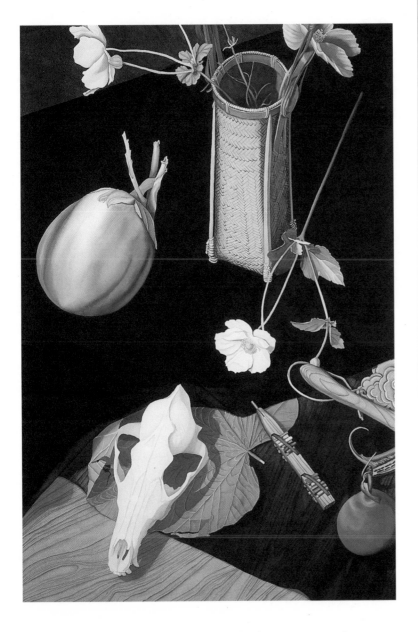

Underpainting

One of the keys to Lisiecki's technique is underpainting a color that has a subtle impact on the ultimate appearance of an object. A wash of cadmium yellow light and alizarin green on the pear before applying the madder carmine, gives the red of the pear a slightly yellow cast.

Shadows

Lisiecki uses mauve to paint the shadows of the green apples, and then applies washes of alizarin green.

Dimension

To give dimension to the red apple, the artist paints the shadows green and then applies washes of madder carmine.

Layers of Color

To distinguish one red from another, Lisiecki paints only some of the fruit with more than one layer of madder carmine. Notice how two or three layers of the red deepen the value and intensity of the color.

Schmincke madder carmine

CAT *Jean Grastorf*, 20" x 28" (50.8 CM X 71 CM)

Color

Mixing

for

Florals

Flowers are some of the most brightly colored objects in nature, so artists who paint them have an opportunity to use intense pinks, purples, reds, yellows, and oranges—often when painting the same blossom! An artist painting florals can use colors full strength without toning them down, making it easier to experiment with the new, strangely named pigments such as quinacridones, iridescents, and metallics.

Achieving that brightness and intensity in a unified composition is not a simple matter. Hot reds and royal blues can be tough to pull together without becoming garish, unnatural, and silly. Sometimes artists have to build up layers of color gradually, ensuring that the different tones work together as the painting develops. At other times, they need to intermix colors on the watercolor paper, making sure the pigments blend without becoming a dull gray.

The three accomplished artists featured in this section offer different approaches to capturing the liveliness of flowers. All three women are quite deliberate about their techniques; this restraint helps them contend with strong color choices.

Susan Headley Van Campen is direct and controlled in her use of floral colors. In painting long green stems, flowing leaves, and delicate blossoms, she mixes several colors together on her palette, and then makes a limited number of brush strokes on the watercolor paper. These combined pigments realistically capture what the artist sees in front of her.

Mary Weinstein selects from many tube colors when she paints the flowers from her garden. She builds up layers of those colors until she achieves the intensity and brilliance of the real blossoms. Weinstein knows how each color will perform by itself and in combination with the other colors.

Jean Grastorf developed a novel approach to watercolor—she pours intense, staining colors across a prepared sheet of paper as if she were dyeing a piece of fabric. As a result, the colors remain clean, transparent, and brilliant. Not every tube color will work, however; Grastorf explains her technique below.

MORNING POND *Jean Grastorf*, 40" x 30" (102 CM x 76.2 CM)

Maximizing Color Mixtures

"I put together strong mixtures of color on the palette and make one stroke to describe each stalk, leaf, and blossom. It's important to be direct when trying to capture the spirit of the flowers growing in my garden."

— Susan Headley Van Campen

Everything about Susan Headley Van Campen's approach to painting flowers in watercolor is deliberate, uncomplicated, and immediate. This observation is especially true of her selection and application of colors. She intermixes a number of pigments on a palette until she gets just the right color and intensity. She then applies that color to the paper with a large brush so it accurately describes the subject in front of her.

"I'm interested in the spirit of flowers as they grow, not in their environment or in their botanical details," Van Campen explains. "I want my paintings to capture their life, not the absolute details of the appearance. Most of the flowers are ones I've grown in my garden because their colors, shapes, and textures appeal to me. The fact that I've been involved in their complete life cycle is important to my paintings of them."

Van Campen emphasizes that color is the most important aspect of the flowers she selects for her garden. She searches for unusual varieties of sunflowers, tulips, irises, and poppies to plant in her garden so the colors will be more interesting than those of the flowers available from florists.

Paintings in this chapter by
Susan Headley Van Campen

(OPPOSITE) PARROT TULIPS 22" X 30" (60 CM X 76.2 CM)
(TOP) GLADIOLUS–AUGUST 22" X 30" (56 CM X 76.2 CM)
(CENTER) VERSCILLAS IN A VASE 22" X 30" (56 CM X 76.2 CM)
(BOTTOM) BLACK IRIS 22" X 30" (56 CM X 76.2 CM)

Getting Started

Ivory Black   Hooker's Green Light   Cadmium Yellow Light   Cadmium Yellow Medium

Viridian   Alizarin Crimson

Winsor Red

French Ultramarine Blue

Winsor Violet   Naples Yellow   Cobalt Violet

Cerulean Blue   Sap Green   Rose Dore   Cadmium Red Light

Cadmium Red Medium

Palette

Van Campen mixes colors on her palette, gradually adding pigments. When painting a leaf, she may start with sap green and add cerulean blue if the leaf has a bluish cast. She doesn't use siennas or umbers, but instead mixes Winsor violet and cadmium yellow medium to capture the browns of nature.

Favorite: *Winsor violet.*

Brushes

Van Campen buys inexpensive Utrecht #12 white nylon sable brushes by the dozen and gives them to her children when they lose their shape.

Favorites: *Utrecht #12 white nylon sable brushes.*

Surface

Van Campen prefers Arches 300 lb cold-pressed paper laid flat on the studio floor or an outdoor blanket. She paints on 22" x 30" (55.9 cm x 76.2 cm) or 40" x 60" (101.6 cm x 152.4 cm) sheets of paper. She doesn't soak the paper or tape it to a rigid surface.

Favorite: *Arches 300 lb cold-pressed paper.*

Van Campen paints as many watercolors as she can during the summer and fall, when her garden is in bloom. She usually lays a blanket on the ground in the garden, spreads her supplies around her, and sits cross-legged on the blanket while she paints. When working from plants in her garden, Van Campen usually paints the stalks all the way to the bottom edge of the paper to suggest growing plants, not cut flowers.

Although she would prefer to paint with the sun shining directly on her paper, Van Campen sits under an umbrella so the glare won't hurt her eyes. She doesn't do any preliminary drawing, preferring just to start painting one flower and move on to the next until she has filled the paper. If the blossoms are likely to change quickly, she paints them before the leaves and stalks. "I only work from life, so I have to adjust to the fact that while leaves may last several days, flowers will change within a period of a few hours as the temperature rises or falls," she explains.

In the winter, Van Campen travels from her home in rural Maine to Boston, where she buys unusual flowers from florists and takes them back to her studio. She then breaks from her normal routine of working on one painting at a time and starts several still-life paintings to get as much done as possible before the cut flowers die.

Maximizing Color Mixtures

◀ 1

Van Campen begins working in her studio from three pots of forced parrot tulips when only three of the blossoms have opened. She uses a transparent mixture of cadmium yellow medium, sap green, Winsor violet, and a little Naples yellow to begin painting the leaves and stems.

▼ 2

After painting three petals with ruffled edges, she goes back to darken some of the edges with a mixture of Winsor red and rose dore. She quickly adds this mixture to introduce a feature of red into each petal.

Prepare strong mixtures of color and paint each part of the flower with one stroke of the brush. Don't go back over the painted shapes unless they seem too weak or the edges are too soft. Your color mixtures will have the greatest impact if you limit yourself to one or two layers of paint.

A mixture of Winsor red and rose dore is added to each petal.

3 ▶

Van Campen now paints more leaves, stems, and buds with a mixture of cadmium yellow, sap green, and Winsor violet. She adds a little French ultramarine blue to the mixture to paint the darker areas. She brushes touches of Winsor red onto the opening of the ruffled buds.

◀ 4

Painting more of the leaves and two sets of petals on the first two tulips, Van Campen uses the same colors that are already on her palette. She mixes these colors again to add a second layer of color on two tulip buds.

5 ▶

Because she is working from living flowers that keep changing, Van Campen makes adjustments to the flowers, opening and bending the first two blossoms and changing one blossom from a green yellow with red flames to a more intense yellow with a pinkish red flame.

6 ▶

The artist uses Naples yellow to add stamens to the flowers. While the paint is still wet, she adds some ivory black mixed with Winsor violet to the tips.

white nylon sable brush

◀ **7**

Van Campen paints more leaves with a mixture of cadmium yellow, cerulean blue, and sap green. She then covers the darker portions of those leaves with a mix of Winsor violet and French ultramarine blue.

Color Mixing Workshop

Combination Greens

Van Campen paints the stems and leaves of the plants with combinations of cadmium yellow, sap green, Winsor violet, and Naples yellow.

To get a darker green, Van Campen adds ultramarine blue to that same combination of colors, as shown in the bottom square.

ultramarine
blue added

Sometimes the "correct" color mixture is the one that performs in a way you personally find to be pleasing. For example, you might

> *Sometimes the "correct" color mixture is the one that performs in a way you personally find to be pleasing.*

select it because the greens flow well when you are painting leaves, or the browns have a warm tone for painting branches, or the color mixture just looks good in your paintings. To discover the color mixture that feels right when you are painting, try all sorts of tube colors and recommended combinations.

After years of painting, Susan Headley Van Campen has developed a sense of which color combinations are "correct" for her paintings of flowers from her garden. Instead of using the raw sienna, burnt sienna, raw umber, or burnt umber to paint tree trunks or branches, for example, she mixes Winsor violet and cadmium yellow medium to make a warm brown.

Van Campen often mixes four or five different tube colors to arrive at the exact green, red, or yellow that she needs for painting branches, blossoms, and leaves. Those mixtures are fluid and intense so that the artist can describe the plant form in one smooth motion of the brush.

Browns

Van Campen doesn't use earth colors—siennas and umbers—because she finds that browns made from combinations of Winsor violet and cadmium yellow medium, such as the ones shown here, are closer to what she observes in nature.

Intense Reds

To describe a flower with one stroke of a brush, Van Campen uses an intense red made from a combination of Winsor red and rose dore.

(OPPOSITE) ZINNIAS AND PEARS–OCTOBER 22" x 30" (56 CM x 76.2 CM)

(TOP) SUNFLOWERS–SEPTEMBER 22" x 30" (56 CM x 76.2 CM)

(BOTTOM) EARLY POPPIES–JUNE 22" x 30" (56 CM x 76.2 CM)

Getting Colors to Work Together

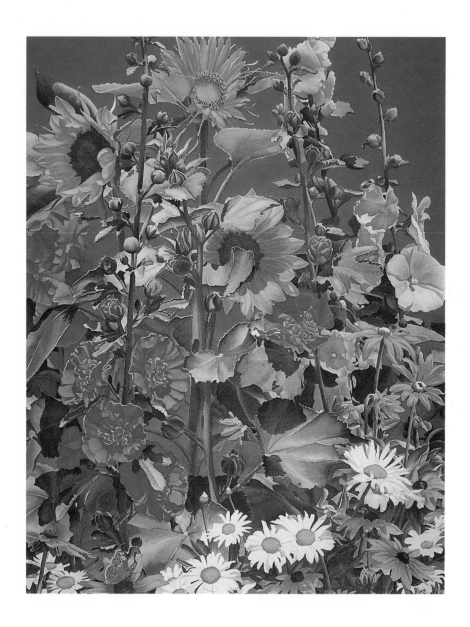

*"Colors have to work together at every stage of a painting's development.
No one color can 'sing' more loudly than the others or be a glaring shape that
doesn't fit in with the rest. I achieve that harmony in the way I mix colors and
glaze them over the ones already on the watercolor paper."*

— **Mary Weinstein**

Mary Weinstein discovered the exciting potential of color in a workshop with the legendary watercolorist Robert E. Wood. Wood showed her how to expand the number of tube colors she used by making sure they worked together harmoniously. That discovery still motivates Weinstein's selection of subject matter, palette of colors, and painting techniques. "I stopped painting the subdued grays that resulted from overworking a few colors, and I started mixing a wide array of related tube colors. Now those color mixtures help me capture the excitement I felt about the colors in my

chosen subject matter," she explains. "As I apply those mixtures to the paper, I make sure they are working in concert with each other."

Weinstein adds, "I begin painting with the colors I see and then glaze mixtures over them. I may start out thinking I'm going to do something soft, and wind up with brilliant pinks and reds; and at other times, I may plan on a strong contrast of darks and lights, and wind up with something subtle."

Quite frequently, Weinstein gets to a point in the painting process where she switches from transparent watercolors to acrylic paints so the colors become even more intense. She seals the watercolors with a light mist of Blair acrylic matte medium, and then applies transparent washes of acrylic paint in a manner that resembles watercolor painting. Because acrylics dry permanently, Weinstein doesn't have to worry that a new layer of color will disturb those underneath it.

Paintings in this chapter by Mary Weinstein

(OPPOSITE) POTPOURRI DES FLEURS 41" X 29 ½" (104.1 CM X 74 CM)
(TOP) WOOD DOOR #17 41" X 29 ½" (104.1 CM X 74 CM)
(CENTER) RASPBERRY SUNDAE 30" X 22" (76.2 CM X 56 CM)
(BOTTOM) LES NYMPHAEA 41" X 29" (104 CM X 74 CM)

Getting Started

New Gamboge   Permanent Rose   Quinacridone Red   Quinacridone Rose   Cerulean   Phthalo Blue

Cobalt   Aureolin   Viridian

Cadmium Yellow

Rose Madder Genuine   Scarlet Lake   Alizarin Crimson   Ultramarine Blue

Cadmium Orange

Palette

Weinstein doesn't have a set palette of colors or a formula for mixing and applying watercolors. The colors shown here represent all of the various hues that might at some point be used by the artist. She starts with a few primary colors and gradually adds pigments. She seldom uses earth colors or tube greens, preferring greens made from combinations of other colors.

Favorites: New gamboge, phthalo blue, phthalo green, and Winsor green.

Brushes

Weinstein uses round brushes in sizes #4, #6, #8, and #12 to paint washes of color. She switches to Robert Simmons synthetic hair brushes when working with acrylic paints.

Favorites: Round brushes in sizes #4, #6, #8, and #12; Robert Simmons synthetic hair brushes.

Surface

Weinstein favors Arches 550 lb rough paper. Because the paper is absorbent, the acrylic paint sinks in and doesn't take on the dull matte finish typical of acrylic colors. She doesn't soak the paper or wipe off the sizing, because she prefers to work on a dry, stiff surface.

Favorite: Arches 550 lb rough paper.

Weinstein works from slides of the flowers in her own garden. She keeps the images in binders so she can select the blossoms needed for a particular painting, often using elements from as many as fifteen different photographs.

She projects the slides onto shapes drawn on watercolor paper, with the pencil lines indicating the size and placement of each flower. She then traces the outlines of the major forms. "In recent years, I've been projecting the photographs even more because that saves time and reduces the strain on my eyes," she explains. She makes print enlargements of the most important slides to use for reference.

Weinstein paints light washes of color to establish the underlying tone of each plant, and follows up with more intense mixtures. She frequently paints several layers of the same color over a shape to achieve the intensity she wants, or alternates two layers of the same color with one that shifts toward a warmer or cooler temperature.

The paper remains completely flat and unstretched while Weinstein paints. If it buckles during the application of large washes of color, she flattens it after the paint has dried by wetting the back, laying it face down between clean sheets of paper, putting a board on top, and applying weights while it dries.

She uses the same palette of colors in acrylics, with the following additions: cobalt violet, Hansa yellow, cadmium scarlet, quinacridone gold, quinacridone crimson, and Jenkins green.

Getting Colors to Work Together

1 ▶

After reviewing photographs of the flowers in her garden, Weinstein draws circles on the Arches 550 lb rough paper and projects the selected images into the shapes indicated by the pencil lines. She then paints the first tints: yellows and new gamboge in every area that will eventually appear yellow, green, or orange; permanent red in other parts of the image; and washes of cobalt blue in the background.

◀ **2**

Weinstein uses cadmium yellow and cadmium orange for the yellow flowers, and scarlet lake, quinacridone red, and quinacridone rose on the blossoms. She paints the sunflower leaves with new gamboge, viridian, and cerulean. The hollyhocks receive the same mix, with a little extra viridian added. Weinstein doesn't preserve any of the white paper because she wants the first tints to be the lightest values. She covers the daisies with new gamboge, viridian, and ultramarine blue.

3 ▶

The artist layers the sunflowers on the left side with cadmium orange glazed over with aureolin; she layers the remaining sunflowers with cadmium orange only. She uses cadmium yellow for the pink hollyhock centers, modeling their form with quinacridone red. Weinstein outlines the daisies with cadmium orange and the leaves with a mix of cadmium yellow, Winsor green, and ultramarine blue.

Mary Weinstein

Weinstein paints the shadows on the yellow flowers with sap green and quinacridone rose; the white ones with cerulean and cadmium orange; the reds with Antwerp blue; and the pinks with cerulean blue. She uses glazes of cadmium yellow and cadmium orange, then applies another glaze of new gamboge. At this point, she sprays the painting with one coat of acrylic matte medium to seal the watercolor so she can apply acrylic paints.

5 ►

Weinstein first paints the red flowers with naphthol crimson. She paints the other reds with quinacridone red; the pinks with permanent rose and, in the shadows, a mix of cadmium orange and viridian. She intensifies the yellow centers with cadmium yellow. Shadows on the leaves are a mix of cadmium yellow, Winsor green, and phthalo blue. The artist brushes in the background with a mix of cobalt violet, cerulean blue, and ultramarine blue.

6 ▶

To finish the painting, Weinstein uses the same palette of colors with the addition of acrylic soft matte medium. She varies the thickness or thinness of the pigment, and glazes over the yellows to increase the intensity. The brown centers of the sunflowers are a mix of cadmium scarlet and Winsor green.

◀ 7

To finish the leaves, Weinstein adds Jenkins green to the darkest areas. She uses cadmium yellow, cadmium red, and Winsor green for the sunflower centers. She then gessoes out the butterfly and repaints it. Weinstein reinforces the background with a deeper mix at the top (ultramarine, pthalo, and cerulean blues), blended with Winsor green and phthalo blue. She glazes over some of the leaves and background to make them blend.

Color Mixing Workshop

Initial Color Washes

Weinstein first paints some flowers with a wash of cadmium yellow and then, when that paint is dry, covers the center with a layer of cadmium orange.

Layers of Red

Here you see how intense the red becomes when Weinstein builds up three layers of red—first scarlet lake, then quinacridone red, and finally quinacridone rose.

Mixtures for Leaves

Weinstein paints this leaf, and many others, with mixtures of new gamboge, viridian, and cerulean blue.

To add variety and dimension to the leaves she paints, Weinstein mixes cadmium yellow, Winsor green, and ultramarine blue.

Of the twelve artists featured in this book, Mary Weinstein has one of the most extensive palettes of both transparent watercolors and acrylic paints. Each color helps her create a certain look, either by itself or in combination with the other colors.

Layering is a critical part of Weinstein's technique. One tube color is painted into a shape, allowed to dry, and then another

> *Layering is a critical part of Weinstein's technique.*

intense and vibrant color is applied over the top. The decision about which color to layer at each stage of the painting's development is based on her judgment of the overall harmony of the picture and on the connection between the real flowers and the two-dimensional depiction of them. Ultimately, the colors have to tell the viewers what Weinstein was feeling about those flowers when they were painted.

After first establishing colors with transparent watercolors, Weinstein will frequently add layers of acrylic paint. Acrylics are water based so they work well with watercolors but they dry permanently and can be built up in thicker, more opaque layers. Weinstein finds that to be advantageous when trying to achieve stronger colors.

She also uses color combinations that are somewhat unusual—like sap green and quinacridone rose.

(OPPOSITE) LES FLEURS DE MON JARDIN 29½" X 41" (74.9 CM X 104.1 CM)

(TOP) GEORGIA ON MY MIND 30" X 40" (76 X 102 CM)

(BOTTOM) FLEURS DU SOLEIL 29½" X 41" (74.9 CM X 104.1 CM)

Shadows

To create the shadows of certain flowers, Weinstein uses a mixture of sap green and quinacridone rose with the yellow flowers, a blend of cerulean blue and cadmium orange with the white blossoms, and Antwerp blue with the red flowers.

Color Mixtures for Flowers

To achieve the color mixtures and layers Weinstein uses in her sunflowers, she mixes new gamboge with viridian and ultramarine blue, and applies them to the paper. She then adds cadmium orange, and applies a wash of aureolin.

Weinstein mixes these colors to create hollyhocks: quinacridone red for the edges of the blossoms; cadmium yellow for the centers; and a mixture of cadmium yellow, Winsor green, and ultramarine blue for the stems.

Pouring Luminous Washes

"With traditional layering techniques, the first washes of color applied with a brush are bright and vibrant, but the successive glazes begin to get dull and muddy. I solve that problem by pouring washes of three transparent, staining colors using specific procedures."

— **Jean Grastorf**

After trying dozens of tube colors and as many painting techniques, Jean Grastorf changed her approach to mixing and simply began pouring washes of three transparent, staining colors on a carefully prepared surface. She masks large shapes and small details, and then pours washes

of those colors. After the first washes of color dry, Grastorf pours a second layer of the three primaries in a manner that resembles batik fabric dyeing. Finally, she does direct painting with a synthetic hair brush to give definition and detail to the image.

The resulting paintings are defined by thin layers of glowing color in a wide range of values and temperatures. Cool, dark purples and blues put the deck rails into deep shadow, while warm, bright yellows and oranges bring the viewer's attention to the sunlit blossoms and curtains. Grastorf allows the watercolor paints to accomplish what they do better than any other medium—to bring life to a subject with a minimal amount of transparent color.

But as simple and carefree as this technique may seem when watching Grastorf at work in her studio, it depends on some specific tools and techniques. During her research, Grastorf found that many colors don't perform well during the pouring process, and that a lack of careful planning and preparation could easily lead to unsatisfactory results.

Paintings in this chapter by Jean Grastorf

(OPPOSITE) SPRING FLOWER 20" x 28" (50.8 CM X 71 CM)
(TOP) SEA GRAPES 30" x 40" (76.2 CM X 102 CM)
(CENTER) BANYAN IV 28" x 20" (71 CM X 50.8 CM)
(BOTTOM) BROMELIAD 20" x 14" (50.8 CM X 36 CM)

Getting Started

DaVinci Phthalo Blue

Cadmium Yellow Deep

Sennelier Cadmium Red Light

Sennelier Red

DaVinci Red Rose Deep

DaVinci Hansa Yellow Light

Holbein Cerulean Blue

Blockx Ultramarine Violet

Palette

Grastorf squeezes paints into round plastic-coated plates that she tosses out after each session. It's important to have fresh color. If the paint dries and you try to reactivate it, you won't get the kind of clean, transparent color you need.

Favorites: *DaVinci phthalo blue, DaVinci red rose deep, and DaVinci Hansa yellow light.*

Brushes

When doing the direct painting, the artist uses synthetic hair Golden Fleece round brushes from Cheap Joe's Art Stuff because they hold a good amount of paint, keep a point, and have a firm snap that she likes.

Favorites: *Round brushes in sizes #6, #8, and #12.*

Surface

Grastorf uses Waterford 300 lb rough paper because of its bright white surface and ability to hold washes. She soaks the paper for ten minutes in a tub of water, staples it to a sheet of Gatorboard, and then tapes around the edges.

Favorite: *Waterford 300 lb rough paper.*

Grastorf works from photographs and sketches to make a value study of the picture. She then creates a full-scale drawing on tracing paper, making any necessary adjustments before transferring the image to a sheet of watercolor paper that she has soaked, stapled to Gatorboard, and allowed to dry thoroughly. At this point, she masks predetermined areas of the paper. The masking agent Grastorf prefers is the Incredible White Mask.

Grastorf dissolves the three staining primary colors in water, preparing stronger mixtures of yellow because the red and blue pigments can overwhelm it. She mixes a large amount of all three paints so she doesn't run out in the middle of a pour.

The artist soaks the prepared paper with clear water, and then pours the three colors across it. She holds the Gatorboard flat so the pigment can soak into the paper, and then pours off the excess. As she pours, she directs the cool colors into the shadowed areas of the picture and the warm colors into the sunlit sections.

When the first layer of color is dry, Grastorf removes frisket from some parts of the painting and applies it to others. She then pours a second layer, adding warm colors over warm colors, cool over cool to maintain harmony and avoid muddy blends. The sections that receive the second wash become deeper and more intense, while those defined by one layer of color remain bright and transparent.

Pouring Luminous Washes

1

A value study helps Grastorf evaluate the large shapes within her still-life arrangement and indicates where she needs to apply the Incredible White Mask before pouring colors across the paper. Using this study and her photographic source material, the artist makes a full-size drawing on tracing paper and refines the shapes within the picture.

photo to help render the still life

2

Grastorf applies the masking agent to the paper to block the back-lit leaves, the purple flowers receiving the sunlight, and the areas that are off-beat in color and require special attention.

ADVICE FROM THE ARTIST

You can add burnt sienna to the palette, but use it only by itself, not mixed with other colors. Also, you can use cadmium yellow deep to warm up an area of the painting, but pour it only once.

3 ▶

The artist lays the Gatorboard flat so she can pour fluid mixtures of DaVinci phthalo blue, DaVinci red rose deep, and DaVinci Hansa yellow light. She gives the mixtures time to stain the paper, and then pours them off. She concentrates the warm yellows and reds in the sunlit areas of the deck and the flowers, and the cool blues and purples in the shadows.

Cool blues and purples are concentrated in the shadows.

◀ 4

After the paper is dry, Grastorf removes some of the dried masking material to expose parts of the white paper. She paints liquid mask over other areas that received the first wash of staining color.

5 ▶

Grastorf again pours the primary staining colors over the paper. She allows the paper to dry completely before removing all the masking material from the watercolor paper.

6

The artist begins the direct-painting process with an expanded palette of colors, using round synthetic hair brushes. She makes a point of applying warm colors over the warm tones already on the paper, and cool colors over the cool tones.

ADVICE FROM THE ARTIST

A gouache mixture can add an interesting contrast to the staining colors. Though I rely on the white of the paper for most of the light values, I use gouache to create some flat matte finish whites.

7

Using the staining color poured in the initial stages as well as the new colors added to her palette, Grastorf continues to add detail. At this point, she doesn't concern herself with the way the actual subject looks in photographs or in life because she wants the picture to have its own reality.

Color Mixing Workshop

Poured Color Washes

Here's a simple demonstration of Grastorf's pouring technique. She blocks the white shapes with the Incredible White Mask and pours the three staining colors (DaVinci Hansa yellow light, DaVinci red rose deep, and DaVinci phthalo blue). When the paint dries, she adds more of the masking agent to preserve the light colors before pouring a second, darker layer of the primaries.

Painted Color Washes

Grastorf then paints washes of color over the initial poured colors, using a synthetic hair brush.

Although Jean Grastorf's color mixing procedures depend on very few tube colors and supplies, they are so different from the others demonstrated in this book that you will want to practice them before attempting a full-scale painting. Do not be surprised if you experience a certain amount of skepticism and anxiety the first time you start pouring diluted paint over the paper. It may seem to be an uncontrollable mess, but with practice you will see how Grastorf is able to get the warm colors in the sunlit areas and the cool colors into the shadows while taking advantage of the random patterns created by the flowing paints.

> *Do not be surprised if you experience a certain amount of skepticism and anxiety the first time you start pouring diluted paint over the paper.*

These are the kinds of simple tests you might want to make to become comfortable with the pouring methods. It will take a few attempts to learn how thin to make the paint, how to tilt the board, and how to exercise a certain amount of control over the results. You will also discover how to anticipate what will happen during the first and second pours, and how you can add detail later with a paint brush.

(OPPOSITE) RHODODENDRON 36" X 45" (91 X 114 CM)
(TOP) BIRD OF PARADISE 20" X 28" (50.8 CM X 71 CM)
(BOTTOM) SUN-KISSED 20" X 28" (50.8 CM X 71 CM)

Poured versus Mixed Colors

The six swatches of color show how Grastorf's palette of primary colors looks when she pours mixtures onto the watercolor paper. Below the swatches are two squares made with the same primaries mixed together on the palette and painted on the paper. Notice how dull and gray the colors become when mixed on the palette and how vibrant they are when poured.

Hansa yellow light & red rose deep
plus, phthalo blue

phthalo blue & red rose deep
plus, Hansa yellow light

THE INN, CLUNES   *Robert A. Wade,* 7" x 11" (18 CM X 28 CM)

Color

Mixing

for

Landscapes

Beginning watercolorists often make the mistake of painting trees with Hooker's green dark, skies with cobalt blue, and rivers with French ultramarine blue. Eventually, they realize that the color of objects in nature depends on the weather and atmosphere, the season of the year, the distance between the observer and the object, and the quality of light. In the middle of August, the grass should probably be painted with a brownish green made from a mixture of yellow ochre, raw sienna, and French ultramarine blue; the sky might best be rendered in a grayish blue made from a combination of cobalt blue and raw sienna; and the rivers would seem more believable if painted with a gray purple made by mixing phthalo blue and alizarin crimson, and painting them on a dampened sheet of paper.

In studying the three artists who contributed to this section, you'll discover ways of understanding and responding to these relative conditions when painting landscapes. Skip Lawrence shows you how to work with strong colors—many of them ones that other artists avoid—to capture your feelings about remembered places. He points out that relative values and intensities are more important than the exact color of the trees and the sky, and shows you how to determine those values.

Robert A. Wade tones the surface of his paper with light washes of color before he starts painting the sky or a river. That tone unifies the picture while it warms the highlights. When Wade is ready to paint the various parts of the landscape, he does so with deliberate, calligraphic brush strokes.

Rolland Golden is more methodical in the way he mixes and applies colors to watercolor paper. He prepares each color uniformly on the palette and applies it evenly to the painting, all in a controlled and carefully considered sequence. He then makes adjustments by glazing over washes of lighter or darker colors.

JANUARY IN VICKSBURG *Rolland Golden*, 30" X 22" (76.2 CM X 55.9 CM)

Emphasizing Color Shapes

"Has anyone ever invited you into their garden to observe the strong pattern of dark and light values? Of course not. They want you to see the colors—and not the puny, soft tones or the dark, flat shadows. They want you to enjoy the deep reds, the brilliant yellows, the glowing whites, and the textural greens."

— **Skip Lawrence**

For most watercolorists, Skip Lawrence's palette of colors and painting techniques are at odds with everything they have been taught. He does not follow the traditional practice of selecting a specific range of pigments and applying them in a sequence—lightest, brightest colors first, then darkest, muted tones. His approach is simple: First, consider the shapes created by the colors you apply to the watercolor paper; then, study the way one color affects the appearance of others in the picture. Finally, work with intense applications of color rather than thin glazes of pigment.

The aim of this unorthodox approach is to create bold, expressive paintings that show what is most exciting in a landscape. To Lawrence, color is the most important element of watercolor painting. It is the key to presenting his response to selected subjects. "Good paintings are the result of clear ideas and honest passion," he says emphatically. "They are expressions of a particular subject that is seen, felt, and understood. Their content (the subject of the artwork) and form (the arrangement of elements) must be considered not as two separate elements of art but rather as one inseparable unit."

Paintings in this chapter by Skip Lawrence

(OPPOSITE) INTRIGUE 22" X 30" (56 CM X 76.2 CM)
(TOP) COMPOSE COMPOSITION 20" X 26" (50.8 CM X 66 CM)
(CENTER) THE EDGE OF ORANGE 29" X 29" (74 CM X 74 CM)
(BOTTOM) GREENVILLE 20" X 26" (50.8 CM X 66 CM)

Getting Started

Permanent Rose

Ultramarine Blue

Compose Green

Jaune Brilliant

Phthalo Blue

Hansa Lemon Yellow

Yellow Ochre

Cadmium Red

Cobalt Blue

Blue Gray

Palette

Lawrence employs up to seventy colors—standard cadmiums, earth pigments, cobalts, and phthalos, plus an array of sedimentary, transparent, and opaque colors.

Favorites: Holbein's compose green and jaune brilliant—toothpaste-thick, opaque colors that are not for purists. He uses them to enhance color intensity and to adjust color relationships, not to correct mistakes.

Brushes

Large, oil painting-style brushes—synthetic or bristle—let the artist control how much water mixes with the paint, and help him move pigment around on the damp watercolor paper.

Favorites: Large #10 and #12 sable brushes; stiff 1 1/2" and 2" bristle brushes; and 2" Skipper brushes for painting backgrounds.

Surface

Rough watercolor paper is best for this technique; paint sinks into the fibers and creates soft edges between forms. Rough paper melts shapes together, whereas hot-pressed paper leaves the edges sharply defined.

Favorites: Arches 140 lb and 300 lb watercolor paper, clipped to a board or, for large paintings, taped down to remain flat.

Before he begins painting, Lawrence makes four or five pencil lines on the watercolor paper to indicate the general shapes that define the basic elements of the picture. Then he dampens the surface of the paper with brush strokes of clean water and applies a diluted wash of color over the entire sheet of paper—usually a warm tone of yellow ochre or cadmium yellow medium. The damp surface is essential to this technique because it allows the color to be thoroughly absorbed into the paper and creates soft edges between the painted forms.

Lawrence does not preserve parts of the white paper for the lightest value in his picture, avoiding the stark contrast of color laid next to the sharp edges of a white shape. Once he applies the washes, his focus shifts to breaking the picture up into a few large shapes using transparent colors like cobalt blue. Then he adds specific elements of the scene—more to balance the relationship of warm and cool colors, bright and gray tones, and intense and subtle pigment dispersals than to add detail.

The landscape shown in the demonstration isn't based on a particular location, but rather on a number of memorable streams where Lawrence has gone fly fishing—it represents more of a feeling than a particular view.

Emphasizing Color Shapes

 1

Beneath a middle-value wash of yellow ochre, a few pencil lines identify the large shapes and directional movements within the picture.

pencil lines beneath wash

 2

While the first color is still wet, Lawrence applies a glaze of cadmium red diluted to the same value as the yellow ochre. "The secret to the successful layering of color is applying washes of the same value and controlling the amount of water on the brush," he explains.

ADVICE FROM THE ARTIST

Try not to get too involved in the small patterns within shapes. Many paintings fail because the artist got lost in painting windows, doors, or branches, instead of the overall relationship of the large shapes.

2" skipper brush for painting backgrounds

Skip Lawrence

3 ▶

The combined washes of yellow ochre and cadmium red make an orange that warms the paper and creates a sense of light. While the paper is still wet, Lawrence applies a glaze of ultramarine blue of the same value. This neutralizes portions of the orange and creates an underpainting for the landscape.

Yellow ochre and cadmium red make an orange that creates a sense of light.

◀ **4**

The artist squeezes a generous amount of transparent, non-staining cobalt blue directly onto the wet paper and smears it around with a 2" Skipper brush to establish a color dominance and mood.

5 ▶

Lawrence adds ultramarine blue, turquoise blue, permanent rose, and small amounts of compose green to the initial shapes in order to contrast with the existing cobalt blue. He introduces the tree trunks using all the previously named colors.

▼ 6

Lawrence adds reflections of color to the stream, and makes the still surface of the water warmer and more neutral with mixtures of complementary and opaque pigments— jaune brilliant, blue gray, and compose green. This develops contrasts with the pure, cool blue of the dominant shape.

When you need an intense color to dominate an area or to act as a bright accent, squeeze the paint directly onto the paper and either brush it in with a 2" Skipper brush or just leave it sitting on the surface.

▼ 7

Hansa lemon yellow, placed above the blue shape to the far left, introduces contrast with the hue and temperature of the blue and harmonizes with the intensity of the hue. The artist slightly darkens the sky shape with a wash of jaune brilliant. From this point on, Lawrence fine-tunes the color relationships with overlays of warm or cool tones, and he adjusts the hard, soft, and broken edges of the various shapes.

Color Mixing Workshop

Value

Value is a critical aspect of Lawrence's work with color. By varying the amount of water you add to paint, you can control the relative value of the color: Lots of water yields light values, and little water yields dark values, as shown in this progressive scale of phthalo blue.

phthalo blue

Colors Mixed to the Same Value

Lawrence stresses the importance of using different colors that have the same relative value. To make values match, you may need to dilute some colors a great deal and others very little. Here, the intense purple hue is diluted quite a bit to match the value of the nearly undiluted brown.

Lawrence says that color decisions at each painting stage are based on personal preferences. "From my experience, I have an intuitive sense of which colors to use," he explains. "I do believe that students need to find out how each color performs alone and with other colors. While my approach to color may be somewhat unorthodox, I still believe an artist needs to know what differences to expect from a cobalt blue, ultramarine blue, and phthalo blue, for example.

"You don't need high contrast between darks and lights to create a successful painting. It can come from an exploration of color relationships, textural contrast, spatial balance, and value shifts." Lawrence also notes that colors get less intense as they sink into the paper and dry. To compensate, it is often necessary to modulate color relationships in the final stages of the painting. One

> *"You don't need high contrast between darks and lights to create a successful painting."*

approach is to dull some colors with an overlay of their complement (a green over a red, for example), and brighten others with a wash of transparent yellow or orange. Opaque colors can be layered to either darken or lighten the values.

Intense Color

Another key element of Lawrence's approach to color is working with intense colors on damp paper. The illustration above was painted with intense, staining colors on wet paper, while the one below was made with highly diluted mixtures of transparent, non-staining colors on a dry sheet of paper.

(OPPOSITE) SUMMER KITCHEN 36" x 45" (91 CM X 114 CM)

(TOP) CARLY 29" x 45" (74 CM X 114 CM)

(BOTTOM) ROAD TO NEW MARKET 29" x 45" (74 CM X 114 CM)

Starting with Tonal Washes

"Painting an initial wash of color over large areas of the watercolor paper
will mellow the pristine whites so the only ones that
remain will accent the objects close to the viewer.
I use this method because there is actually very little true white in nature."

— **Robert A. Wade**

A key aspect of Robert A. Wade's approach to watercolor is washing color over large portions of the paper and going back with strong linear marks of mixed colors to define the elements of the landscape. He applies those strong colors in confident and deliberate calligraphic strokes. "Never will my brush strokes be timid," he says. "If I don't quite know what to do next, I will do nothing until I am positive I have made the right decision, which I will put into effect with confidence."

The Australian artist follows a rather traditional approach to watercolor in that he usually paints from light to dark values, from thin to thick mixtures of paint, and from broad areas to smaller details. But his technique varies in the initial stages of the process because he doesn't save much of the white paper. "In the initial stages of the painting, I like to cover the sheet with washes of raw sienna, cobalt blue, or touches of light red as soon as possible, working in big, soft, light-valued shapes and then going back into some of them wet-in-wet," he explains. "I will require the paper to dry after this stage is over, then I can go into layering and, finally, defining some shapes with more intense color mixes, using ultramarine blue or alizarin crimson in combination with other colors to give a thicker, dark mix. I try to achieve a variety of soft and hard edges, with some dry-brush effects for contrast."

Paintings in this chapter by Robert A. Wade

(OPPOSITE) TUMUT TRACK 15" X 20" (38 CM X 51 CM)
(TOP) THE CHARLES, PRAGUE 15" X 20" (38 CM X 51 CM)
(CENTER) THE WALL OF CHINA 15" X 20" (38 CM X 51 CM)
(BOTTOM) SPIRES OF PRAGUE 14" X 10" (36 CM X 25 CM)

Getting Started

Winsor Violet

Alizarin Crimson Permanent

Burnt Sienna

Quinacridone Gold

Light Red

Aureolin

Raw Sienna

French Ultramarine Blue

Phthalo Green

Cerulean Blue

Permanent Magenta

Cadmium Yellow

Cobalt Blue

Permanent Rose Quinacridone

Cadmium Red

Raw Umber

Phthalo Blue

Palette

Wade uses about three times as much cobalt blue as any other color because it mixes so well with other pigments to create beautiful grays, greens, mauves, and subtle browns that are transparent and non-staining. He also mixes raw sienna with other colors to make excellent grays and greens.

Favorites: Cobalt blue and raw sienna.

Brushes

He prefers Robert A. Wade signature white nylon brushes (available only in Australia): 1¹/₂" flat and #6, #8, #12, and #16 rounds. He also uses Winsor & Newton Series 7 kolinski round sables in all sizes from #4 through #14.

Favorites: Robert A. Wade white nylon brushes.

Surface

Wade usually works with Arches, Lanaquarelle, Fabriano, Bockingford, or David Cox paper.

Favorite: Waterford, because he likes the way it accepts washes of color and releases them if the values need to be lightened.

Wade tapes his paper to a board, rubbing the tape so it won't lift. He never soaks the paper, but frequently wets specific areas with clear water using a flat brush. In his studio, the artist works at a custom-made painting desk illuminated by lights that approximate sunlight; when outdoors, he uses a portable easel. Wade stands while painting because it allows him to step back to evaluate the developing image.

Using his quick studies and compositional drawings, Wade sketches in the basic outlines of the shape he intends to paint, and then brushes on heavily diluted mixtures of colors that cover most of the paper. For example, he might use a pale wash of raw sienna in the sky area to establish a warm underpainting for the blue, which he adds while the wash is still wet.

In the initial stages, Wade develops light-valued shapes. He builds up four or five washes of color in an area, keeping each wet so the transparency of the colors isn't lost. He then allows the paper to dry before defining the shapes with stronger mixtures of color and calligraphic brush marks.

Having traveled around the world almost thirty times, Wade is accustomed to working under all kinds of conditions. He finds his palette of colors versatile enough to capture the light and atmosphere of landscapes from Morocco to Maine.

Starting with Tonal Values

 1

Wade completes this 6" x 9" (15.2 cm x 22.9 cm) watercolor study and the pencil drawings of the cattle on location in five or ten minutes. He takes photographs of the same scene and brings the sketches and photographs back to his studio, where he uses them as reference material for the large watercolor.

pencil sketches done on location

Wade prefers a white nylon brush

2 ▶

The artist paints a pale wash of raw sienna across the entire sky area. He also brushes in the soft clouds wet-in-wet with cobalt blue and a touch of light red, which turns the blue into a warm gray. Using mixtures of cobalt blue and permanent magenta, he adds the distant hills to the damp, lower portion of sky color.

3

Continuing to work down the sheet of paper, Wade applies a warm mixture of light red and raw sienna over the track. He also paints a bright, warm wash of quinacridone gold on the shapes of the cattle, making sure to preserve some white highlights on the animals.

ADVICE FROM THE ARTIST

Let your feelings about a subject guide your selection of colors. If you sense a warm glow, use the bright yellows on your palette. If you are moved by the dark, cool shadows, then mix in the darker blues and purples.

 4

Wade adds trees with a transparent mixture of raw sienna and cobalt blue, building up texture without focusing on detail. He uses a green made by combining cobalt blue and raw sienna to create a dark pattern under the cattle.

Cobalt blue is mixed with raw sienna to make a dark green shadow.

5

Looking more closely at the cattle, Wade uses stronger mixtures of quinacridone gold, raw sienna, and cobalt blue to give weight and mass to the animals and their cast shadows. Washes of permanent magenta and Winsor violet establish the cast shadows of the trees.

Quinacridone gold, raw sienna, and cobalt blue add weight to the cattle.

6

Wade continues to work on the forms of the cattle, darkening the values with mixtures of French ultramarine blue, alizarin crimson, and a touch of burnt sienna. He alters the shape of the puddle and adds a small amount of off-white gouache to restore the crisp edge on the dark cow.

Color Mixing Workshop

Raw Sienna Wash

Wade often begins a painting by laying a wash of raw sienna over his preliminary drawing to establish a warm tone to the colors applied later.

raw sienna

cobalt blue

Cobalt Blue Wash

Occasionally, he applies a wash of his other favorite color, cobalt blue, either by itself or mixed with raw sienna.

At one time it was quite common for watercolorists to work on sheets of paper that were lightly colored by the manufacturer. A tint of tan, blue, or green served as a ground that gave the first washes of watercolor a warm or cool tone, and it necessitated the use of Chinese white or white gouache for the lightest values in a composition. Eventually, those papers were replaced by the pure white papers used today. In recent years a few manufacturers have reintroduced the tinted sheets of paper.

> *Robert A. Wade finds it useful to have a light wash of color covering his watercolor paper.*

Robert A. Wade finds it useful to have a light wash of color covering his watercolor paper, but instead of buying sheets manufactured with uniform tones, he paints large areas of his paper with thin mixtures of raw sienna or cobalt blue after his drawing of a subject is complete. Those tones help to unify the composition, and because value is relative, Wade can make those tints seem as light as the white of an untinted sheet of watercolor paper. He does that by keeping the tints thin and making the darks within the picture quite strong. The contrast between those darks and the tints is sufficient to make an effective composition.

(OPPOSITE) Hangin' Out, Venice 15" x 20" (38 x 51 cm)

(TOP) In Scudamore's Barn 15" x 20" (38 x 51 cm)

(BOTTOM) The Green Awning, Bruges 11" x 14" (28 x 36 cm)

Clouds

Wade applies cobalt blue over a wash of raw sienna to make the clouds. Below are swatches of raw sienna and cobalt blue, along with the mixtures of cobalt blue and light red used in the clouds, and the cobalt blue and permanent mauve combination painted along the hillside.

Trees

In painting the trees, Wade uses combinations of cobalt blue and raw sienna to make several dark greens. Here he paints those green mixtures over a wash of cobalt blue.

Controlling Color Washes

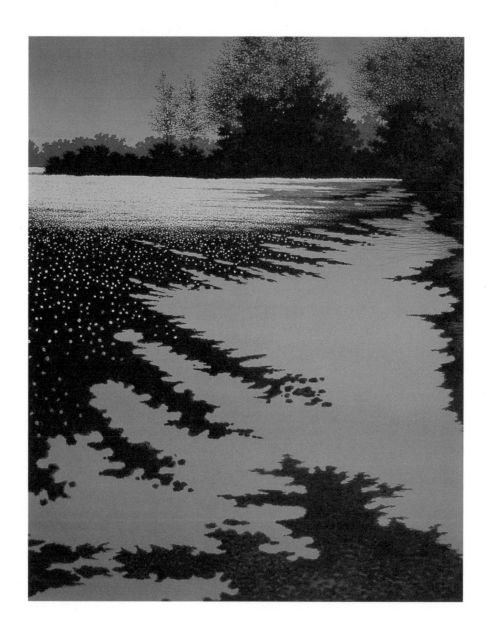

"The key to getting a consistent, even wash of color is to mix plenty of paint, test the intensity of the pigments and the overlapping washes, and stir the mixture thoroughly before each stroke of the brush."

— **Rolland Golden**

Rolland Golden describes himself as a "control painter," in that he measures, plans, tests, and organizes every aspect of his creative process. His watercolors express exactly what he intends because he thoughtfully plans the composition and the colors. Golden carefully chooses his pigments and applies them to the paper in uniform washes that are usually confined to hard-edged shapes. He also follows certain time-tested procedures for

mixing colors. For example, he first dilutes the weaker pigments like cobalt blue and yellow ochre with relatively small amounts of water, and then gradually adds the stronger pigments like Antwerp blue and cadmium red. He tests the combination on a scrap of the same paper used for his picture, either by itself or washed over other colors on his palette. These procedures make it possible for Golden to work with colors that other artists avoid, such as Prussian blue, an intense, staining color that can easily overpower weaker pigments.

Although Golden's slow, methodical technique doesn't lend itself to being taught in workshops or demonstrations, he is generous in sharing information about the way he uses color in an organized, carefully planned manner. "I personally feel it is more satisfying to create the painting you imagine in your mind rather than one that just happens on the paper. For that reason, I like to have a compositional plan established before I begin to paint and a fairly clear idea of how each new color I apply will affect the evolving painting."

Paintings in this chapter by Rolland Golden

(OPPOSITE) SOUTHERN ICE 33" X 25" (83.8 CM X 63.5 CM)
(TOP) HOLY ROLLS 22" X 30" (55.9 CM X 76.2 CM)
(CENTER) ST. CAGNÉ SUR MER 25" X 18" (63.5 CM X 45.7 CM)
(BOTTOM) WORK IN PROGRESS 35 ½" X 26 ½" (90.2 CM X 67.3 CM)

Getting Started

Payne's Gray

Cadmium Red Light

Cadmium Red Medium

Naples Yellow

New Gamboge

Burnt Sienna

Antwerp Blue

Indian Red

Sepia

Yellow Ochre

Prussian Blue

French Ultramarine Blue

Cobalt Blue

Burnt Umber

Raw Umber

Cadmium Yellow Medium

Palette

Golden places a glass palette over a white sheet of paper for mixing colors because it allows him to judge the transparency and intensity of the pigment. He usually mixes one combination of colors at a time unless he intends to apply two separate mixtures and blend them together on the paper.

Favorite: Burnt sienna.

Brushes

The choice of brushes is important to Golden's ability to manage the broad washes of color and tight edges. Most of his brushes are round and made from sable because sable holds a large amount of color and releases it gradually.

Favorites: Kolinski sable brushes in sizes #2 to #12.

Surface

Golden buys paper in rolls and cuts it to size. He always dampens the paper to remove the sizing. While the paper is still wet, he staples smaller sheets to boards and larger sheets to wooden canvas stretchers. The paper becomes tight and flat as it dries.

Favorite: Arches 240 lb cold-pressed paper.

Golden uses on-site sketches or photographs as source material for the small black-and-white sketches he makes to determine how he will organize the values and shapes within a picture. He may create several of these sketches before finalizing the proportions of the painting, the composition of forms, and the application of colors.

He then draws the image in the sketch on the stretched watercolor paper in a freehand manner, carefully defining every shape. Golden sometimes leaves a white border between the drawing and the edge of the stretched paper so he can use that space to test colors before applying them.

One of the distinguishing characteristics of Golden's paintings is the seamless uniformity of the washes he lays on the paper. Achieving that kind of wash depends on applying even pressure on the brush, connecting one stroke of color with the next, and maintaining the consistency of the paint. Golden makes sure he mixes up plenty of paint before applying a wash, and he stirs the paint before each brush stroke so the pigment is evenly suspended in the water. He also tilts the painting slightly so gravity will help to pull the colors down the paper as he applies each stroke of paint.

Controlling Color Washes

1

Golden projects a slide photograph of his subject onto a sheet of paper. He makes a pencil drawing of the landscape to determine the relative value of each section and to make notations about the colors he will use. According to Golden, this method "returns me to the scene."

2

Golden draws the outlines of the landscape forms in pencil, and masks out the white shapes in the cotton fields and some of the tree leaves using Maskoid. He then applies a wash of cobalt blue and Prussian blue for the sky and water, and blocks in the background trees with French ultramarine blue, raw umber, and Prussian blue. He paints the leaves with yellow ochre, cadmium yellow, and Antwerp blue.

 ## 3

After painting some of the darkest green leaves with a mixture of Prussian blue and sepia, Golden removes the Maskoid from the sky. He adds colored leaves on the right side with a combination of cadmium red, burnt sienna, cadmium red light, and cadmium yellow. When he paints cadmium red medium over the blue sky, the resulting color is a rich crimson.

Rolland Golden

 4

Golden removes the Maskoid from the trees on the left and paints in some leaves. Using a combination of burnt umber, French ultramarine blue, raw umber, and sepia, he lays a flat wash of color over the foreground and middle ground. He then adds a deeper burnt sienna to the tree along the right margin and paints the dark green trees in front of it.

> ### ADVICE FROM THE ARTIST
>
> *Try to find a specific reason why you want to paint a subject and make sure that everything you do is aimed at showing the viewer what that reason is. Carefully consider the composition of the picture, the choice of colors, and the sequential application of washes.*

5

Using sepia and burnt umber, the artist paints another layer of color over the middle ground and edge of the mud to the right. He then places a wash over the bottom area using yellow ochre, raw umber, burnt umber, and Antwerp blue. At this point, he removes the remaining Maskoid.

6

Golden eliminates or reshapes many of the cotton ball shapes to establish variety and depth in the picture. He paints shadows across the fields with a mixture of French ultramarine blue, Payne's gray, and Antwerp blue to give the impression of late afternoon light. The artist then decides to remove the yellows from the distant trees by placing a thin wash of red over the existing yellow.

ADVICE FROM THE ARTIST

Take advantage of the natural opacity of colors like Naples yellow, cadmium red light, cadmium red medium, and cerulean blue. Thick mixtures of those colors can help you add texture or lighten an area.

7

Golden finishes the painting by adding some variations along the bottom using yellow ochre, raw umber, burnt sienna, and Prussian blue. He reduces the contrast in the brown tree on the right and lowers the brightness of the distant red trees by adding more leaves with cadmium red medium and burnt sienna. Golden adds dark limbs to the closest cotton plants and reinforces the darkest black green.

Color Mixing Workshop

Blended Sky

Golden creates a sky color by blending Prussian blue and cobalt blue.

Alternative Colors

Artists often find alternatives to their favorite colors when a manufacturer discontinues the color, the pigment proves not to be lightfast, or a similar color might perform better. For example, Rolland Golden's favorite color is burnt sienna, shown below on the left, but he can use the new Rowney transparent oxide red, shown on the right, when he wants a staining, non-sedimentary color that looks similar.

burnt sienna / transparent oxide red

Dramatic changes have been taking place in the manufacturing of watercolor paints, with many colors being completely eliminated or replaced by combinations of different pigments that approximate the appearance of the original colors. Sometimes this is due to the lack of quality raw materials, to the environmental problems caused by the manufacturing process, and to consumer pressure to use pigments with higher lightfast ratings.

Two of Rolland Golden's favorite colors (burnt sienna and alizarin crimson) are still readily available as professional grade, high-quality watercolor paints, but they are among the colors that other artists are substituting on their palettes. Those artists are finding inconsistencies in the quality of burnt sienna, and they are concerned about using certain brands of alizarin crimson that haven't received the highest lightfast rating.

Pointillist Technique

Rolland Golden uses a pointillist technique of painting small, independent spots of color that blend together in the viewers' eyes. Here are three examples of how the same green made by combining Prussian blue and cadmium yellow looks completely different when painted over burnt sienna, a dark blue (French ultramarine blue, raw umber, and Prussian blue), and two layers of green (yellow ochre and cadmium yellow, both mixed with Antwerp blue).

burnt sienna & burnt umber

yellow ochre, cadmium yellow, & Antwerp blue

French ultramarine blue, raw umber, & Prussian blue

So while there is nothing wrong with using the same palettes of colors as Rolland Golden or any of the other artists featured in this book, you may someday find it necessary to consider alternatives when a favorite paint either changes or becomes unavailable.

Winsor & Newton alizarin crimson (discontinued)

Winsor & Newton permanent alizarin crimson

Winsor & Newton quinacridone red

Daniel Smith perlyene scarlet

Deep Reds

Alizarin crimson is a deep, versatile red, but watercolorists are finding alternatives for it because the pigment is not completely light-fast. The first swatch of color shown above is the discontinued Winsor & Newton alizarin crimson, and the second is the lightfast substitute the company now offers. The next two swatches are other alternatives to alizarin crimson: Winsor & Newton quinacridone red and Daniel Smith perlyene scarlet.

mauve (discontinued)

Winsor violet

ultramarine violet

Mauve

Mauve is another color that manufacturers are discontinuing. The first swatch shows a true mauve, the others show Winsor violet (dioxazine) and ultramarine violet, suggested alternatives.

(TOP) THREE'S A CROWD 25" X 35" (63.5 CM X 88.9 CM)
(BOTTOM) OUTLIVED & OVERGROWN 25½" X 34" (64.8 CM X 86.4 CM)

NENE—HAWAIIAN GOOSE *Jeremy Pearse*, 7 ½" X 11" (19 CM X 28 CM)

Color

Mixing

for

Wildlife

Details are of utmost importance to artists painting wildlife subjects, so their approach to color must allow them to achieve accurate renderings of feathers, fur, and leather. Wildlife artists need to select tube colors that match the colors on real animals, and they must apply the colors to the painting in controlled brush strokes. But the need for precision doesn't mean the presentation has to be flat, dull, or boring. With a vibrantly colored background, a lively setting, or a focused depiction, the colors of animals can be as captivating as those of flowers or landscapes.

The three artists featured in this section all concern themselves with scientific accuracy in their depiction of animals. They rely heavily on the earth colors—siennas, umbers, and ochres—as well as on the various colors of gray. These watercolorists also depend on thoughtful planning, concise rendering, and cautious painting of one section at a time. They carefully consider each color mixture and brush stroke.

Jeremy Pearse mixes lots of water with earth colors like raw sienna, raw umber, and yellow ochre so he can wash thin layers of paint on sheets of hot-pressed paper. This approach allows him to build up the colors gradually until they accurately record the appearance of the birds that have captivated him since childhood.

Sharon Weilbaecher uses the techniques she learned as a medical illustrator to mix natural colors for the ducks in her paintings. Her secret is "floating" the color onto dampened sections of the watercolor paper. By first moistening the paper with clean water, she is able to glide the paint over her precise drawings.

Colleen Newport Stevens begins her paintings by following some of the same procedures used by Weilbaecher for rendering animals. Stevens then washes brilliant, rich colors into the background to lend a distinctive excitement to her finished paintings. That step helps her create award-winning new paintings or revive ones that she had previously abandoned.

FOX SPARROW *Jeremy Pearse*, 22" x 15" (56 CM X 38 CM)

Detailing with Thin Washes

"I need to be in complete control of the painting process, so I work slowly, building up multiple thin washes of color, and stopping often to assess what I have just completed. That helps me accurately record what I observe in nature."

— Jeremy Pearse

Although British-born Jeremy Pearse enjoys looking at all the colors in nature, he is only interested in painting the subtle grays, browns, ochres, reds, and blues in wildlife. "I'm as captivated as anyone else by the red feathers on a male cardinal or the pink plumage on a flamingo, but I am seldom moved to paint those bright colors," he explains. "I'm more interested in the subtle relationships of muted, harmonious colors. Those seem to convey my feelings about the birds I have observed all my life."

To achieve that balance of colors, Pearse starts painting with thin mixtures of the colors he observes in nature, and slowly builds the form of the bird with layers of closely related pigments. He may begin with a mixture of yellow ochre and raw sienna, add a small amount of raw umber to those colors for the next layer, and then mix in a touch of cadmium red for the third wash. He continues this process until he feels the representation of the bird is accurate.

"I don't start out with a value sketch that tells me how dark or light something needs to be or how intense the pigments should appear," he comments. "I arrive at those decisions as I am painting the animal. That process works well for me, particularly since I am painting on a hot-pressed paper that is unforgiving."

Paintings in this chapter by Jeremy Pearse

(OPPOSITE) GREAT HORNED OWL 7" X 10½" (18 CM X 27 CM)
(TOP) CRESTED SNAKE EAGLE 7" X 10½" (18 CM X 27 CM)
(CENTER) HARRIER AT BLACKWATER 10½" X 7" (27 CM X 18 CM)
(BOTTOM) SAURUS CRANE 13½" X 9" (34 CM X 23 CM)

Getting Started

Aureolin   Cadmium Red Medium   Raw Umber   French Ultramarine Blue

Winsor Red   Cobalt Blue

Cadmium Yellow Medium   Indian Red

Raw Sienna   Yellow Ochre   Sepia

Burnt Sienna   Burnt Umber   Cerulean Blue   Neutral Tint

Palette

Pearse doesn't include any tube greens on his palette because he prefers to mix his greens from combinations of blues and yellows, modified with small amounts of earth colors. He occasionally uses permanent white gouache to lighten values or add fine details.

Favorites: *Raw sienna, raw umber, cobalt blue, and neutral tint.*

Brushes

Pearse prefers synthetic hair brushes to those made from animal fur. He use fairly large sizes, #6, #8, and #10, even when painting small areas. He does have some old natural hair brushes, including a Chinese Sumi-i brush his wife once used, for painting small details.

Favorites: *Synthetic hair brushes.*

Surface

Pearse prefers Arches 140 lb hot-pressed paper stretched on a board. The paper takes some getting used to, so Pearse recommends practicing on scrap sheets before beginning a painting.

Favorite: *Arches 140 lb hot-pressed paper.*

Most of Pearse's subjects are in the fields or zoos near his home, so it is relatively easy for him to study, make sketches, and take photographs of the wildlife he might want to paint. He occasionally makes preparatory drawings, but more often than not simply gathers his materials together and begins painting a subject. "I've been studying birds since I was eight or nine years old, and I know when something looks correct or it doesn't," he explains. "I can usually tell from the very beginning of the painting process whether or not a painting will be successful. If it's likely not to be, I tear the piece up and begin again. I'm really ruthless in that regard."

Pearse does almost all of his paintings on Arches 140 lb hot-pressed paper, which he stretches. It took him a while to get used to the hard, smooth surface and the slow rate of absorption, but the paper allows him to paint finer details and achieve the subtle color relationships he finds so important.

Referring to his sketches and photographs, Pearse does a light but detailed drawing of his subject on the paper, and then begins the painting process. His Winsor & Newton paints are spread out in the compartments of a plastic palette with a mixing area in the middle. He mixes small amounts of color with generous amounts of water as he begins painting, reducing the amount of water as he nears completion of the work.

Detailing with Thin Washes

aureolin and cadmium
yellow for the eye

 1

Pearse does a light, detailed drawing of the great horned owl, and applies two thin mixtures of raw sienna, raw umber, and neutral tint to the background. He then adds some aureolin and cadmium yellow medium to the bird's eye; raw sienna and burnt sienna to the lightest area of the plumage; and neutral tint to the darkest parts of the eye.

2 ▶

The artist washes Indian red into the area below the eye and aureolin yellow into the eye itself. He uses a mixture of neutral tint, raw umber, and burnt sienna to indicate warmer shadows just above the eye, and adds a little more burnt umber to the mixture to outline the eye.

3 ▶

Pearse doesn't think the eye is dark enough, so he adds another wash of aureolin to the iris, then burnt umber to the shadow. He paints a mixture of aureolin, raw sienna, and raw umber in the background, and defines the lower edge of the base of the bill with a gray-brown wash.

Pearse adds another wash of aureolin to darken the eye.

◀ **4**

With neutral tint, Pearse darkens the bill, the ear coverts, and the markings on the crown. He adds a mixture of raw sienna, raw umber, and burnt sienna to the crown and, after diluting it with more water, to the cheek and ear tufts. The dark quarter-moon shape surrounding the ear coverts receives multiple washes of neutral tint.

5 ▶

Pearse washes cerulean blue over the bill and completes the ear tufts with darker washes of raw sienna and raw umber. Neutral tint helps define the feathers and separates the lower edge of the cheek and the darker feathers below. On the back of the head, Pearse paints a thin mixture of the same brown used earlier.

6

The artist uses a mixture of raw sienna, raw umber, and cadmium red to indicate the palest coloring on the breast and the lower side of the head. He paints the intricate vermiculations on the side of the head with neutral tint and sepia, and some of the darker areas with burnt umber.

ADVICE FROM THE ARTIST

If you want a dark area of the painting to have depth and richness, paint it first with a wash of burnt umber.

7

Pearse applies a few more washes of neutral tint to establish the final details, and adds one last wash of raw sienna to the breast.

Color Mixing Workshop

Muted, Harmonious Colors

To achieve the muted effects that Pearse prefers, he works with closely related earth colors mixed to the same relative value. In fact, Pearse avoids painting animals that would require him adding bright oranges, greens, or blues to his palettes.

raw sienna

raw umber

neutral tint

neutral tint

burnt sienna

sepia

neutral tint

Dramatic changes do not occur from one stage to the next when Jeremy Pearse creates one of his remarkable wildlife paintings. The shifts from one color mixture to another are achieved with the addition of a small amount of pigment, and the changes from one layer of paint to the next are as subtle as Pearse can make them. He will work with the same three or four colors for days, adding a little more raw sienna for one section of a painting, a bit more cadmium red for the next, and a small amount of neutral tint for the third.

Seeing Pearse's subtle color combinations as separate swatches will give you a better sense of how he works with these pigments to achieve the tight details, soft surfaces, and personal interpretation that make his paintings so successful. Remember that Pearse paints on hot-pressed paper, which responds to the color mixtures quite differently than cold-pressed paper.

(ABOVE) HORNED OWL AT DUSK 8" X 11" (20 CM X 28 CM)
(OPPOSITE TOP) GYRFALCON 7½" X 11" (19 CM X 28 CM)
(OPPOSITE BOTTOM) SAW WHET OWL 22" X 15" (56 CM X 38 CM)

Warm Mixtures

Pearse varies his color palette by using warm mixtures of color to paint both his wildlife subjects and the environments in which they live.

raw sienna

raw umber

cadmium red

aureolin

indian red

Floating Colors onto Damp Paper

"I mix colors with small amounts of water on a palette and then float them into shapes on the watercolor paper already dampened with clear water. I also use an airbrush to spray controlled mists of color."

— **Sharon Weilbaecher**

Trained as a medical illustrator, Sharon Weilbaecher has an approach to color mixing that is different from other artists, in that she develops one small section of a picture at a time after first making a detailed pencil drawing. "Medical illustrators are expected to render accurate details and deliver their finished paintings by a deadline, so they learn painting methods that achieve accuracy, and develop salvage techniques for making changes," she explains. The proce-

dures she employs help her use color to establish an accurate depiction of a subject within an expressive painting.

The most critical part of Weilbaecher's technique is floating colors into shapes drawn on the watercolor paper that have already been dampened with clear water. She first mixes those colors with small amounts of water on a dispos- able wax paper palette, pulling in the paints that she has squeezed around the mixing area. As she floats the mixtures onto the damp paper, the colors sink in and become soft shapes that blend with the shapes around them.

In later stages of the painting process, the artist applies colors on the dried surface of the

paper to depict details, or she draws linear features with colored pencils. She frequently uses an airbrush to achieve the realistic appearance of objects or to unify a background. That tool, powered by a compressor, sprays a controllable mist of color onto the sections of the paper that have not been blocked by cut stencils or liquid frisket.

Paintings in this chapter by Sharon Weilbaecher

(OPPOSITE) LADIES OF THE LAGOON 26" X 36" (66 CM X 92.4 CM)
(TOP) SOUTH OF THE RAINBOW 30" X 22" (76.2 CM X 55.9 CM)
(CENTER) THE LURE OF FISHING 27" X 26" (68.6 CM X 66 CM)
(BOTTOM) MORNING CUP 39" X 28" (99.1 CM X 71.1 CM)

111

Getting Started

Winsor Blue   Ultramarine Blue   Brown Madder Alizarin   Raw Umber

Cadmium Red   Cadmium Orange   Sepia   Raw Sienna

Warm Sepia   Cadmium Yellow Pale

Burnt Sienna   Winsor Red   Alizarin Crimson   Yellow Ochre   Winsor Yellow

Palette

Weilbaecher relies heavily on the transparent, staining colors (Winsor blue, Winsor red, and Winsor yellow) because they can be mixed to make bright, clean colors or floated over previously painted colors to change their appearance.

Favorites: Winsor red, Winsor yellow, Winsor blue, cadmium red, cadmium yellow, yellow ochre, and brown madder alizarin.

Brushes

Weilbaecher prefers Winsor & Newton Series 7 kolinski sable brushes in sizes #00, #0, #1, #2, and #3 for painting details and #4, #5, #6, and #8 for floating colors over larger areas; and Robert Simmons 2" synthetic hair brushes for laying in washes.

Favorites: Winsor & Newton Series 7 in sizes #0, #1, #4, and #5.

Surface

The artist uses Arches 300 lb cold-pressed paper because it can withstand scrubbing when an area of color needs to be lightened or removed.

Favorite: Arches 300 lb cold-pressed paper.

Weilbaecher carefully plans her painting before preparing a palette of colors. She explains, "Using photographs of my subject, I make sketches of the elements I am considering, cut the sketches out, and move them around on a clean sheet of paper to determine where they should be placed. Once that is determined, I make a value drawing. Then I draw the final image on a sheet of watercolor paper, taking a considerable amount of time to record all the details."

Weilbaecher sprays a workable fixative over the pencil lines so they won't be disturbed by the washes of color. She soaks the paper, staples it to a board, and allows it to dry. Then she dampens one section of the paper and floats mixtures of staining colors.

If an area of a painting needs texture, Weilbaecher splatters colors from the end of a brush while covering the rest of the picture. She also uses an airbrush to spray color into sections of the paper masked by hand-cut frisket paper or liquid frisket. And if she wants finer details or sharper edges, she adds them with colored pencils.

Weilbaecher's training in medical illustration helped her develop techniques for altering areas of a painting. For example, she uses a nylon fingernail brush to scrub colors off of one section. After the paper is thoroughly dry, she smoothes the surface with fine sandpaper.

Floating Colors onto Damp Paper

1 ▶

After working out her composition on a sheet of Strathmore drawing paper, Weilbaecher enlarges and transfers the image to a sheet of Arches 300 lb cold-pressed paper, and carefully draws the details of the ducks and landscape. She then sprays the pencil lines in the ducks with a light mist of workable fixative.

◀ **2**

After soaking the watercolor paper, stapling it to a board, and allowing it to dry, Weilbaecher paints sepia watercolor over the lines of the drawing. Next, she dampens the paper in the area of the ducks' wings and floats a wash of Winsor blue over them.

3 ▶

The artist dampens the paper for each duck (leaving the light areas dry) and floats a warm wash of raw sienna mixed with yellow ochre. She floats some cadmium orange on the bills and feet, and then lets the paper dry. Finally, she floats warm sepia on the shadow side and a hint of burnt sienna on the wing.

Sharon Weilbaecher

 4

Weilbaecher applies liquid frisket to the leaves, twigs, and stones with a small brush, and then floats a combination of Winsor blue, Winsor red, and a small amount of Winsor yellow. While the ground area is still damp, she floats burnt sienna and Winsor blue in a small spot of the foreground. Once the paper is dry, she splatters burnt sienna, Winsor blue, raw sienna, and burnt umber using a bristle brush.

5 ▶

Weilbaecher now directs her attention to each of the ducks, floating washes of raw sienna, yellow ochre, and cadmium orange with a little cadmium red on their bills. She leaves the white of the paper for the highlights and applies thick mixtures of colors to the dry paper to capture the details of the feathers.

white paper highlights

◀ **6**

After applying liquid frisket to the outline of the ducks next to the shoreline, the plants, and the cypress knees, she floats separate washes of cadmium yellow pale and Winsor blue. Removing the frisket, she then adds further details to the ducks using washes of raw sienna, yellow ochre, and Winsor blue. She softens some edges by wetting the paper and rubbing it with a cotton swab.

▼ 7

The artist wants to strengthen and darken the blue behind the ducks' heads, so she cuts frisket paper to cover the ducks and sprays colors with a Paache double-action airbrush powered by a Badger compressor. She sprays Winsor blue behind the ducks, cadmium yellow in parts of the water, and burnt sienna and Winsor red in the tree and leaves.

Floating colors gives them a softer appearance because they sink into the paper, lose their hard edges, and leave the paper smooth and absorbent. When the paper is dry, you can use thicker mixtures of color to paint details over those soft colors.

▼ 8

Weilbaecher decides to remove the plants in the background by scrubbing the paper with a nylon fingernail brush. When the paper is dry, she smoothes it with fine sandpaper. She then floats washes of Winsor blue, ultramarine blue, burnt sienna, and Winsor red into that area. She adds reeds with gouache paint and lightens the foreground in value by scraping the paper with a single-edged razor.

Color Mixing Workshop

Without Fixative

Weilbaecher spends a great deal of time drawing the ducks in her painting, so she sprays them with a light mist of workable fixative. This first illustration shows what would have happened if she hadn't applied the fixative— the pencil lines dissolve with the first wash of watercolor.

With Fixative

Weilbaecher sprays this drawing with workable fixative, so the pencil lines remain visible through the sepia color painted to further reinforce the lines.

Colored Pencil

Weilbaecher uses colored pencils to apply more colors over the drawing and sepia lines.

Sharon Weilbaecher uses a wider range of tools and materials than most artists because her training in medical illustration has acquainted her with a number of special techniques for adding color to a developing picture. For example, she is the only artist in this book who uses an airbrush to spray a light mist of color into the background of her wildlife painting.

She is the only artist in this book who uses an airbrush to spray a light mist of color into the background of her wildlife painting.

She demonstrates a way of removing part of the painted image by sanding and filing off some of the watercolor paper.

Other special techniques that Weilbaecher uses include spraying a drawing with workable fixative, scratching lines into the surface of the watercolor paper with a craft knife, drawing lines with colored pencils, and painting dry-brush details. All of these are tools with which the artist can create the believable appearance of her subject—whether it is a duck, a chicken, or a human being. Note that Weilbaecher's color mixtures are applied over a careful drawing made from reference photographs and sketches, an essential guide through the first few stages of the painting process.

Scratching

To keep the linear look to the feathers, the artist employs colored pencils over the watercolor washes, and then scratches lines into the paper with an X-acto knife.

Mixtures of Primary Colors

This chart shows the variety of mixtures that can be made by combining some of Weilbaecher's favorite colors: Winsor blue, Winsor yellow, and Winsor red.

(OPPOSITE) AUNT MOTHA 21" X 29 ½" (53.3 CM X 74.9 CM)
(TOP) SUNDAY MARKET 28" X 30" (71.1 CM X 76.2 CM)
(BOTTOM) WAITING IN NEPAL 39" X 28" (99.1 CM X 71.1 CM)

Mixing Intense, Bright Colors

"I learned to control watercolors by using
only a few transparent, non-staining
colors and then gradually added intense
colors to my palette. I found those strong
colors maintained their brilliance
if I mixed them on the
painting, not on the palette."

— **Colleen Newport Stevens**

In the competitive arena of wildlife art, Colleen Newport Stevens has distinguished herself by using brilliant reds, purples, and golds to capture the vitality of her subject matter. In most of her paintings, she paints a single animal naturalistically with washes of transparent watercolors, and then infuses the background with brilliant colors from other water-soluble paints and crayons. She introduces these other media to establish a contrast in the surface texture of the painting while bringing excitement to the play of colors.

"Once I have established the contrasts of light and shadow with transparent watercolors, I can add more color with watercolor, acrylics, inks, watercolor crayons, and pastels," Stevens explains. "Those paints allow me to control, change, and enhance an image. Furthermore, I create another type of contrast in the textures."

These color combinations have proven so effective that Stevens has repainted older pictures to make them more exciting. A few washes of scarlet lake, quinacridone gold, or alizarin crimson acrylics or inks in the background of those landscapes and wildlife paintings give them new life.

Paintings in this chapter by Colleen Newport Stevens

(OPPOSITE TOP) CROWNED GLORY 22" X 30" (56 CM X 76.2 CM)
(OPPOSITE BOTTOM) THE THINKER II 30" X 22" (76.2 CM X 56 CM)
(TOP) DEEP END 22" X 30" (56 CM X 76 CM)
(CENTER) FEET ONLY A MOTHER COULD LOVE
    22" X 30" (56 CM X 76 CM)
(BOTTOM) THE FLAMINGO 30" X 22" (76.2 CM X 56 CM)

Getting Started

Aureolin

Quinacridone Gold

Manganese Blue

Alizarin Crimson

Scarlet Lake

Phthalo Blue

New Gamboge

Cobalt Blue

Rose Madder Genuine

Viridian

Phthalo Green

Palette

Stevens cautions that although painting with intense colors can create exciting pictures, you must control those pigments. When using phthalo colors, for example, she often finds it necessary to mix them with other colors to keep them from "screaming." Her acrylic palette includes those colors plus cadmium yellow medium, cadmium red light, azure blue, royal blue, and purple brilliant.

Favorite: *Scarlet lake.*

Brushes

The artist uses 2" and 3" Daniel Smith synthetic hair flat brushes for laying in the initial washes, and synthetic and natural hair rounds in sizes #6 and #8 for making calligraphic strokes and rendering details.

Favorites: *2" Daniel Smith synthetic hair flat brushes.*

Surface

Stevens favors Lanaquarelle 300 lb cold-pressed or rough paper because of its bright white surface, and Arches 300 lb rough or cold-pressed paper because it can take a lot of scraping, lifting, and layering of color. She finds the rough papers absorb colors better.

Favorites: *Lanaquarelle and Arches 300 lb rough paper.*

Stevens works from her own photographs of animals. She makes freehand drawings of her subjects on watercolor paper attached with large Bulldog clips to sheets of Gatorboard. She then puts the mounted paper on an easel so she can stand while painting.

Stevens squeezes her watercolor paints into two palettes. When working with Pebeo acrylics, she puts those around the edges of a white enamel butcher's tray. When she first began painting with watercolors, Stevens followed the recommendations offered by Jeanne Dobie in her book, *Making Color Sing* (Watson-Guptill Publications, Inc.). She learned more about color and design from Christopher Schink and Milford Zornes.

After three years of mixing aureolin, rose madder genuine, viridian, cobalt, and new gamboge to create award-winning paintings, Stevens began using more intense, staining colors like scarlet lake, alizarin crimson, and phthalo blue. She also began to mix her colors directly on the painting surface. "When mixed on the palette, the stronger colors can be overpowering and may cause a mixture to become muddy and gray. They are easier to control and maintain their vitality when applied wet-in-wet on the watercolor paper," she explains. "It also helps to keep the painting surface in a vertical position so the colors flow down the paper and interact with each other. Those techniques help keep the colors exciting."

Crowned Glory

 1

After drawing the crowned crane from her own photographs, Stevens begins painting with a palette of transparent watercolors. She mixes cobalt blue and scarlet lake with generous amounts of water to make a dark purple that she washes onto the rough watercolor paper.

2

Washes of new gamboge, aureolin, and rose madder genuine fill in the background with bright, transparent colors. These colors become the underlying tone of the intense reds, yellows, and purples applied over them.

 3

Stevens uses Rotring inks and Pebeo acrylic paints to create a brilliant background. Because these paints dry permanently, she can build layers of color until she gets the intensity she wants.

The Thinker II

1 ▶

Referring to photographs she took at the zoo, Stevens makes a freehand pencil drawing of the gorilla. She then begins to establish the contrast of light and shadow on the animal using transparent, non-staining colors. She mixes those colors—cobalt blue, rose madder genuine, and aureolin—to create a gray color directly on the rough watercolor paper.

contrast of light and shadow created with transparent, non-staining colors

 2

Continuing with a palette of transparent pigments, Stevens paints a background of bright colors to suggest a jungle. She prefers not to refer to the zoo environment because it is so unnatural.

ADVICE FROM THE ARTIST

Learn to work with color by limiting yourself to a few tubes of paint that can be mixed to make a complete array of colors. The five colors I began with were aureolin, rose madder genuine, viridian, cobalt, and new gamboge.

3

Now working with Rotring inks, Stevens darkens the background and the body of the gorilla. She uses intense mixtures of purple for the shadowed areas.

4

Pebeo acrylic colors allow her to change the foliage in the background completely and introduce some yellows, bright greens, and reds into the jungle. She draws dark lines around the animal with Caran d'Arches pencils to help separate it from the background.

Color Mixing Workshop

Watercolor Dyes & Liquid Acrylics

One of the techniques Stevens uses to get intense color in her background is to apply watercolor dyes and liquid acrylics over washes of transparent watercolor. The colors, which are quite intense and brilliant, can be applied with the droppers attached to the caps of the bottled paint or with paint brushes. Here is a sample of two of the brightest watercolor dye colors.

Colleen Newport Stevens uses various color combinations, managing powerful pigments like scarlet lake and phthalo blue as well as subtle colors like aureolin, viridian, and rose madder genuine. The key to her success is using one palette of colors for an animal placed at the center of her watercolor paper, and another selection of colors for the background.

That intense, atmospheric background is a feature that helps distinguish Stevens's wildlife paintings from those created by other artists. These bright colors are not easy to mix because they tend to dominate any pigment they are combined with. After a little experimentation, you could use these colors to liven up your paintings—even unsuccessful ones you have already tossed aside.

sunshine yellow and permanent crimson — brilliant concentrated colors

Scarlet lake   alizarin crimson   phthalo blue

Outside: aureolin, new gamboge, and rose madder genuine

Center: cobalt and scarlet lake

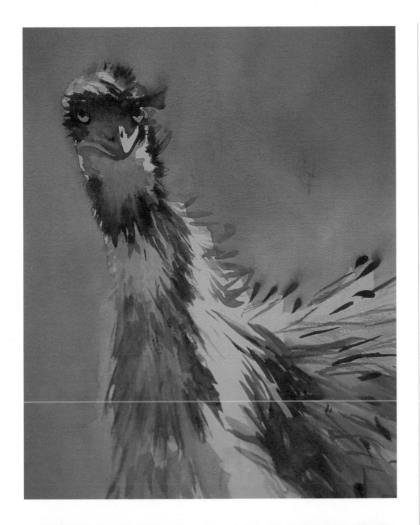

Using Liquid Acrylics

Liquid acrylics can also be dropped into a background to make it more vibrant. They will dry permanently, so subsequent washes of color will not disturb them. Here an opaque yellow was painted and allowed to dry before a deep brilliant red acrylic paint was applied over the top.

yellow gold opaque acrylics — deep brilliant red acrylic paint

(TOP) EMU 28" X 22" (71 CM X 56 CM)

(BOTTOM) THE GATHERING 22" X 30" (56 CM X 76.2 CM)

Color

in the

Studio

Imagine your sixth-grade English teacher saying "Here are the rules of grammar. Now feel free to break them," or your college science professor encouraging you to circumvent the scientific method. If you were pursuing the study of English or Biology, the results would be disastrous. With watercolor painting, however, breaking the well-established rules and techniques for mixing and applying colors produces exciting and refreshing results—new colors and new techniques to help you find your own unique voice as a creative watercolorist.

This section reconsiders some of the tried-and-true watercolor techniques and characteristics to come up with the best color combinations for a painting in development. Artists need to know the recommended ways of mixing colors and applying them to watercolor paper. Rules about intensity and value, washes, color-lifting, brush techniques, color blooms, and combining mediums don't have to be absolute, however. Learn how to break the rules to stimulate your search for creative and effective color mixtures, and to keep your painting fresh and original.

Controlling Intensity and Relative Value

Thin layers of color mixtures work together when all of them have the same relative intensity and the values are balanced.

Intense colors are just as effective depicting a subject. Stronger mixtures are used to create the same kind of landscape, but in this case the relative values are much closer.

Even when the color mixtures are changed radically, their relative intensity and value still affect the outcome of the painting.

Sometimes the right color mixture won't produce a successful watercolor painting because the colors don't work well together on the paper. A glowingly transparent green made from aureolin yellow and cobalt blue may look great on the palette but appear weak if placed next to a strong brown made from burnt umber and ultramarine blue. The difference between the intensities and relative value of those two color combinations is too large.

Artists such as Deborah L. Chabrian and Jeremy Pearse work with subtle differences between the intensity and relative value of their color mixtures. Others, such as Jean Grastorf and Rolland Golden, strive for sharp contrasts between light and dark shapes.

Some teachers tell their students that the "rules" of watercolor require them to work with thin mixtures of color, while other instructors dictate the use of intense colors. Ultimately, the best rule to follow is to balance your color mixtures to suit your subject matter and personal style.

Making value sketches before you begin painting is one effective way to determine the composition of values in your painting, and making color swatches of your mixtures before you apply them to the paper will give you confidence in the intensities of those combinations.

Flat and Graded Washes

When colors are mixed thoroughly with lots of water, they can be applied to watercolor paper in uniform, flat washes or in graded bands of blended tones. These carefully painted washes are great for creating the appearance of cast shadows, rounded still-life objects, or broad skies.

The "rules" concerning flat and graded washes call for a generous amount of color prepared in advance, with the watercolor paper slightly elevated along its top edge, and the colors applied with horizontal strokes of a well-charged brush.

For a more textured wash or more color variation, you can break the rules by mixing the colors directly on the surface of the paper or applying the prepared color mixtures in random strokes of a brush.

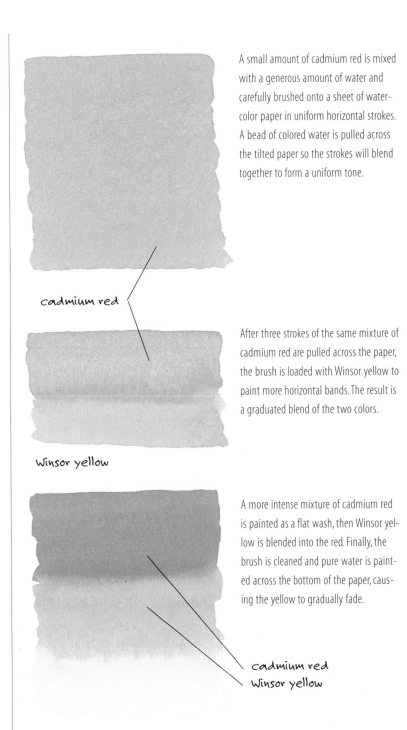

cadmium red

Winsor yellow

cadmium red
Winsor yellow

A small amount of cadmium red is mixed with a generous amount of water and carefully brushed onto a sheet of watercolor paper in uniform horizontal strokes. A bead of colored water is pulled across the tilted paper so the strokes will blend together to form a uniform tone.

After three strokes of the same mixture of cadmium red are pulled across the paper, the brush is loaded with Winsor yellow to paint more horizontal bands. The result is a graduated blend of the two colors.

A more intense mixture of cadmium red is painted as a flat wash, then Winsor yellow is blended into the red. Finally, the brush is cleaned and pure water is painted across the bottom of the paper, causing the yellow to gradually fade.

Lifting Color

Step 1

Step 3

Step 2

Step 4

STEP 1: After painting a leaf shape with a mixture of phthalo blue and Winsor yellow, blot the wet surface with a facial tissue to create a random texture. Note that the Winsor yellow comes through in the blotted areas.

STEP 2: Paint the veins of the leaf over the texture surface using the same color mixture, phthalo blue and Winsor yellow.

STEP 3: To create lines in the leaf shape, blot a wet mixture of cobalt blue and permanent yellow with the folded edges of a facial tissue.

STEP 4: To emphasize the lines previously lifted off the watercolor paper, go back over the leaf with brushstrokes of the same color mixture.

Blotting the edges of a painted shape produces a soft, irregular look quite different from the one created with a brush.

To imitate the appearance of marble, velvet, or stone, lift color from a freshly painted area.

Touching the surface of freshly painted color with a paper towel, soft cloth, or facial tissue softens edges, lightens values, and creates interesting textures. The great American watercolorist Charles Demuth almost always blotted the wet surfaces of his paintings to emphasize the flat, textured appearance of his still-life subjects.

If you blot a shape painted with a combination of staining and nonstaining colors, it's likely you will remove more of the nonstaining color, thus allowing the staining color to show more clearly. To lift color with more control, use a clean, damp paintbrush. That technique creates the impression of a rounded form or produces a soft transition between shapes touching each other.

There are a number of unorthodox techniques for lifting color. One is to sprinkle table salt into a wet area so the grains of salt will absorb the paint and create a speckled texture. Another is to lay plastic wrap over an area of wet paint to create a texture without lifting too much paint.

Wet-in-Wet and Dry-Brush

When one fluid mixture of color is applied to another already on the watercolor paper, the technique is referred to as wet-in-wet painting. As the colors blend together and dry, the edges of the painted shape become soft. That's especially useful when you want a subtle transition between colors to create the appearance of a leaf, a piece of fabric, or the fur of an animal.

Dry-brush painting techniques are perfect for adding final details, sharpening the edges of shapes, or creating a randomly patterned texture in a rendering of tall grasses. As the name implies, dry-brush applications depend on the colors being mixed with a minimal amount of water so they are intense and opaque. To create thin lines, apply the color mixtures with a thin round brush. For a rough pattern, use a wide brush to make the dry-brush marks that will skip across textured watercolor paper.

The "rules" of watercolor say you can't correct mistakes, but dry-brush techniques allow you to paint over areas that aren't quite successful. Because the color mixtures are opaque, they can lighten dark values, sharpen soft edges, and conceal objects that don't work in the composition.

Wet-in-wet blends of color create the soft edges of rounded forms.

permanent yellow

phtalo blue

transparent oxide red

Lifting color after painting a wet-in-wet blend also establishes a dimensional appearance.

Wet-in-wet blending can produce textures, as in this case, where Winsor yellow and transparent oxide red are painted into a wash of cadmium red.

A wide brush is used to create a dry-brush texture across the sky, and a thin brush loaded with thick paint makes the tree shapes along the bottom.

Color Blooms

To create color blooms, drops of clear water are released into the upper left-hand and lower right-hand corners of a square of wet green paint.

cadmium red

Cadmium red is dropped into a flower shape painted with clear water to make a color bloom that resembles a spidery blossom.

Blue and green color mixtures are allowed to flow together across a dampened rectangular shape, forming an intriguing pattern of fluid shapes.

The very idea of working a color bloom into a painting is at odds with watercolor conventions, yet it is a way of celebrating the flowing, transparent, random character of the medium. Color blooms, or back washes, are generally considered mistakes because they are an uncontrollable breakup of the color mixtures. But there may be times when you want to use those "mistakes" to emphasize the natural flow of the watercolors.

One way to create color blooms is to drop clear water into freshly painted areas, causing the wet pigment to pull back and collect along the edges of the randomly patterned shape. Another method is to drop color into areas previously painted with clear water so that the color will flow into the dampened areas of the paper. A third technique is to drop one color mixture into a freshly painted second color.

While the patterns created with these techniques can be random, you can exercise a certain amount of control over the color blooms by varying the amount of paint, waiting until the first layer of color is nearly dry, or tilting the paper in one direction or another.

Combining Mediums

Purists will tell you the "rules" of watercolor dictate creating paintings entirely with transparent watercolor, never adding opaque watercolor, acrylic, colored pencil, or other "foreign" materials. But in recent years there has been an explosion of interest in the special color mixtures that can be achieved with the use of those other supplies.

Opaque watercolor (or gouache) is a water-soluble paint that has more opacity than regular transparent watercolor. It can be used to lighten values, add white accents, or correct mistakes. Acrylics, also water-soluble, can be applied to watercolor paper in opaque, translucent, or transparent washes that dry permanently. Use acrylics to create varieties of textures, densities, and finishes in paintings, or even as adhesives when applying collage materials.

To add finishing details to a watercolor or to create a resist, use wax-based colored pencils. Create interesting visual effects by drawing lines with colored pencils and then applying washes of watercolor—the watercolor won't cover the waxy lines.

Lines are drawn with a wax-based colored pencil and then covered with a wash of Winsor yellow and French ultramarine blue. The wax resists the watercolor paint, allowing the lines to show through.

French ultramarine blue

Winsor yellow

Cadmium red acrylic paint is applied over a square of French ultramarine blue watercolor. The transparent acrylic dries permanently and will not be reactivated by additional strokes of watercolor paint.

cadmium red

French ultramarine blue

Yellow gouache paint is applied over French ultramarine blue watercolor. Because the gouache is opaque, it covers most of the blue. Both colors would be reactivated by additional strokes of either gouache or watercolor.

yellow gouache

French ultramarine blue

The Best Greens

Cobalt blue + aureolin:
A transparent green
perfect for glazing.

Cobalt blue + Winsor
yellow: A cool green
for distant trees.

Phthalo blue + permanent
yellow: An intense, cool
green for bright plumage or
sunlit grasses.

Antwerp blue + Winsor
yellow: A subdued,
cool green for pears
and apples.

French ultramarine blue
+ Winsor yellow: A warm,
light green perfect for
foreground foliage.

The color green, above all other hues, provokes the most discord among watercolorists. Some artists insist that the only compatible greens are those made from combinations of blues and yellows. Through her pouring technique, Jean Grastorf combines DaVinci phthalo blue and DaVinci Hansa yellow light to make the green color in her paintings. Tube greens, they argue, are garish and inconsistent with other colors on their palette. But just as many watercolorists find those tube greens—permanent green light, sap green, alizarin green, and phthalo green for example—to be far easier to work with than the mixed greens.

The truth is that the best greens are those you find most comfortable to work with. If, like Deborah L. Chabrian, you prefer a simple palette of colors that can be intermixed to give you every color you need, then you won't need tube greens. But if, like Mary Weinstein, you prefer an extensive palette of all the pigments you might possibly use, then stock up on all the tube greens available.

Keep in mind that some greens are cool and work best when used to suggest distant trees, shadowed plants, or hidden leaves; other warm greens are better suited to creating the appearance of sunlit leaves, foreground plants, or highlighted fruit.

French ultramarine blue + quinacridone gold: A warm, olive green for fields of grass.

Hooker's green light: A transparent, non-staining tube green for soft landscape forms.

Alizarin green: A crisp, bright tube green for glazing over still-life objects.

Winsor green: A permanent, staining tube green perfect for inclusion in a limited palette.

Contributors

DARYL BRYANT studied with Millard Sheets in Claremont and at the University of Southern California before traveling to Italy to work, paint, and study. She earned a degree in graphic design, and worked as an art director, muralist, sculptor, printmaker, and illustrator before devoting herself to watercolor painting. An early teacher, Verna Wells, inspired her initial enthusiasm and love of watercolor. She credits her further growth as an artist to her mentor and instructor, master painter Joseph Mendez. She has participated in workshops taught by Mendez, Judi Betts, Marilyn Simandle, Milford Zornes, and Gerald F. Brommer. Her paintings have appeared in juried exhibitions and commercial galleries in California.

Daryl Bryant

1136 Fremont Avenue, Suite 101

South Pasadena, CA 91030

DEBORAH L. CHABRIAN studied at the School of the Art Institute of Chicago before graduating from Parsons School of Design. She later took courses at the School of Visual Arts in New York and studied privately with Burton Silverman. Her paintings have won awards and have been included in juried shows organized by the National Academy, National Watercolor Society, American Watercolor Society, Catherine Lorillard Wolfe Art Club, and Society of Illustrators. She is an artist member of the National Watercolor Society, Catherine Lorillard Wolfe Art Club, and Kent Art Association.

Deborah L. Chabrian

28 Spooner Hill Road

South Kent, CT 06785

ROLLAND GOLDEN graduated from the John McCrady Art School in New Orleans and became a full-time professional artist nearly

forty years ago. He is a member of the Watercolor U.S.A. Honor Society, National Arts Club, National Watercolor Society, Allied Artists of America, National Society of Painters in Casein and Acrylics, Rocky Mountain National Watermedia, Audubon Artists, and Louisiana Watercolor Society. His paintings have been featured in a number of books and magazines, including *The World of Rolland Golden*, *American Artist* magazine, *Watercolor* magazine, *International Fine Art Collector* magazine, *Southwest Art* magazine, *Louisiana Life* magazine, and *New Orleans* magazine. His works have also been included in dozens of solo and group exhibitions organized by the Mississippi Museum, Butler Institute of American Art, Deland Museum, National Arts Club, and other notable institutions.

Rolland Golden
78207 Woods Hole Lane
Folson, LA 70437

JEAN GRASTORF is a signature member of the American Watercolor Society, National Watercolor Society, and Florida, Montana, Midwest, Southern, and Georgia watercolor societies. She has been featured in *The Artistic Touch* by Chris Unwin, *Painting in Harmony with Nature* by Maxine Masterfield, *Artistic Touch 2* by Chris Unwin, and *Splash III, Splash IV,* and

Splash V by Rachel Wolf. Her work has been shown at the National Academy of Design. She has won awards in the Rocky Mountain National Watermedia Exhibition and the Adirondacks National Exhibition of American Watercolors. Grastorf often juries art shows and teaches workshops demonstrating her technique of pouring luminous washes. Her watercolors are included on the Artscape Internet site at http:\\www.artscape.com.

Jean Grastorf
4th Avenue North
St. Petersburg, FL 33710

WILLIAM B. (Skip) LAWRENCE was born and educated in Baltimore, Maryland. He received a bachelor's degree of fine arts at

the Maryland Institute College of Art and a master's degree of arts at Towson State University. He is a signature member of the American Watercolor Society, the Southern Watercolor Society, and the Baltimore Watercolor Society. He authored the book *Painting Light & Shadow in Watercolor* (North Light Publications, Inc.) and is the co-author of *Watermedia Focus*, a quarterly instructional publication sold through Cheap Joe's Art Stuff (800-227-2788).

Skip Lawrence

5000 Old Barthololows Road

Mount Airy, MD 21771

DENISE LISIECKI received a bachelor's degree of fine arts from Miami University in 1973 and a master's degree of arts from the State University of New York at Oswego in 1975. Her paintings and prints have been widely exhibited and collected. Lisiecki's artwork can be found in the collections of the Hickory Museum of Art in Hickory, North Carolina; Kalamazoo Institute of Arts in Michigan; Jesse

Besser Museum in Alpena, Michigan; and Dunnegan Museum of Art in Bolivar, Missouri. She is represented by the Jerald Melberg Gallery in Charlotte, North Carolina; Robert Kidd Gallery in Detroit, Michigan; and Bonfoey Gallery in Cleveland, Ohio. Lisiecki is the chairman of the two-dimensional art department and director of education at the Kalamazoo Institute of Arts.

Denise Lisiecki

3210 East G Avenue

Kalamazoo, MI 49004

JEREMY PEARSE was born in Devon, England, and lived in South Africa and Hong Kong before moving to Gaithersburg, Maryland, in 1993. His paintings have been included in major art exhibitions, including the Mid Atlantic Wildfowl and Wildlife Festival in Virginia Beach, Patuxent Wildlife Show in Maryland, Hudson River Wildlife Festival in New York, and Birds in Art exhibitions at the Leigh Yawkey Woodson Art Museum in Wausau, Wisconsin. He is an elected member of the Society of Animal Artists. Pearse is represented by the McBride Gallery in Annapolis, Maryland; Trotman's in Winston-Salem, North Carolina; Massachusetts House Galleries in Maine; and Broadway Gallery in Falls Church, Virginia.

Jeremy Pearse
P.O. Box 2324
Gaithersburg, MD 20886-2324

COLLEEN NEWPORT STEVENS received a bachelor's degree of fine arts from Eastern Washington University in Cheney, Washington. Her paintings have received awards in exhibitions organized by the Midwest Watercolor Society and the Louisiana Watercolor Society. They have been included in Watercolor USA (1994, 1995), organized by the Springfield Art Museum in Missouri, and Birds in Art (1995, 1996, 1997), organized by the Leigh Yawkey Woodson Art Museum in Wausau, Wisconsin. Her watercolors have been published in issues of *Watercolor Magic* and *American Artist* magazines. Stevens is represented by Madison Avenue Art Gallery in Germantown, Tennessee, and Anacortes Gallery in Washington.

Colleen Newport Stevens
8386 Meadow Run Cove
Germantown, TN 38138

SUSAN HEADLEY VAN CAMPEN studied at Moore College of Art and the Pennsylvania

Academy of the Fine Arts, both in Philadelphia. Her paintings are included in major private, corporate, and museum collections, including those of the Readers Digest Association, the Woodmere Art Museum, the Delaware Art Museum, the Federal Reserve Bank, and George Lucas. Her works have also been reproduced in magazines and newspapers, such as *American Artist*, *Down East*, and the *Maine Sunday Telegram*. They have also been included in the books *Painting Flowers* (Watson-Guptill Publications, Inc.), and *A Woman's Journal* (Running Press). Van Campen is represented by the Clark Gallery in Lincoln, Massachusetts; Gross McCleaf Gallery in Philadelphia; Priscilla Saunders Gallery in York Harbor, Maine; and Pandion Gallery in Fishers Island, New York.

Susan Headley Van Campen

39 Knox Street

Thomaston, ME 04861

ROBERT A. WADE was born in Melbourne, Australia, where he still resides. He has gained international acclaim as an artist, with his watercolors winning over a hundred awards. His work has been included in shows organized by the Royal Watercolour Society and the Royal Institute of Painters in England; the Knicker-bocker Artists, American Watercolor Society, and Salmagundi Club in the United States; and the Australian Watercolour Institute in Australia.

He was elected Artist of the Year by the Victorian Artists' Society in 1985 and 1986, and received the Advance Australia medal in 1986. He has written two books for North Light Publications: *Painting More Than the Eye Can See* and *Painting Your Vision in Watercolor*. Wade teaches painting and study workshops around the world.

Robert A. Wade

Dunoon, 524 Burke Road

Camberwell, Victoria

3124, Australia

SHARON WEILBAECHER, formerly of Fort Smith, Arkansas, now lives in New Orleans, Louisiana. She received her bachelor's degree of fine arts from the University of Colorado and her master's degree of arts in medical illustration from the Johns Hopkins University in Baltimore.

 She has published over 800 medical illustrations. Her paintings can be found in many private and corporate collections.

Sharon Weilbaecher

31 Plover Street

New Orleans, LA 70124

MARY WEINSTEIN is a retired real estate broker. She studied painting with Robert E. Wood, Scott More, and Linda Stevens, and attended the Laguna Beach School of Arts. She is a signature member of the National Watercolor Society and Watercolor West, and has served as a vice president of both organizations. Her paintings can be found in many private and public collections, including the San Bernardino Country Museum and Redlands Community Hospital.

Mary Weinstein

35917 Deerbrook Road

Yucaipa, CA 92399

Index

About the Author

M. STEPHEN DOHERTY is editor-in-chief of both *American Artist* and *Watercolor*
magazines. He graduated summa cum laude and Phi Beta Kappa from Knox College
in Galesburg, Illinois, and earned a master of fine arts degree in printmaking
from Cornell University. He is the author of numerous magazine articles and books, including
*Dynamic Still Lifes in Watercolor, Developing Ideas in Artwork, Business Letters for Artists,
Creative Oil Painting,* and *The Watson-Guptill Handbook of Landscape Painting.*
Doherty frequently judges art competitions, offers lectures and critiques,
and exhibits his own paintings and prints. He is represented by the Bryant Galleries
in New Orleans, Louisiana, and Jackson, Mississippi.